A WORLD OF SOURCES II

A WORLD OF SOURCES II

SOURCES II

FURTHER INSIGHTS FROM A LIFE OF READING

Michael J. Hillyard

iUniverse, Inc.
Bloomington

A WORLD OF SOURCES II
FURTHER INSIGHTS FROM A LIFE OF READING

iUniverse books may be ordered through booksellers or by contacting:

iUniverse
1663 Liberty Drive
Bloomington, IN 47403
www.iuniverse.com
1-800-Authors (1-800-288-4677)

ISBN: 978-1-4620-6119-8 (sc)
ISBN: 978-1-4620-6120-4 (ebk)

Printed in the United States of America

iUniverse rev. date: 10/22/2011

ABOUT THE AUTHOR

Michael Hillyard is an education and training consultant. He has served as a dean, provost, president, trustee, and director of various colleges and universities. Hillyard was educated at Miami University (Ohio), American Military University, and the University of Southern California, where he received his doctorate in public administration. He lives with his family in Florida.

OTHER BOOKS BY MICHAEL HILLYARD

A World of Sources: Insights from a Life of Reading

Cincinnatus and the Citizen-Servant Ideal: The Roman Legend's Life, Times, and Legacy

Homeland Security and the Need for Change: Organizing Principles, Governing Institutions, and American Culture

Public Crisis Management: How and Why Organizations Work Together to Solve Society's Most Threatening Problems

"Great things have small beginnings."

—Sir Francis Drake

TABLE OF CONTENTS

adopting the method for their own purposes. At some point in my journey as a reader, I not only read books, but I also found myself taking notes in the margins of the books I read, underlining key passages, and otherwise enjoying a "conversation" with their contents. After employing this process with many books, it became impossible to keep track of the books I had read when I wanted to later reference their insights. So, I started to capture each book's insights by transcribing the underlined passages and margin notes and storing those insights in a binder. Although time consuming, I can now review the (now several) binders' contents and refresh my thinking with important insights whenever I desire to do so. The binders bulge with insights from several hundred books and provide the source material for this book.

The third reason I wrote the books is to enable others to benefit from the knowledge I gained without having to spend thousands of hours reading all of the source material. Readers can read these books and then spend the rest of their time applying their insights and reading other books of interest to them.

A final reason I wrote the books is in knowing that I will learn much in the authorship process of compiling the sources, reviewing what I thought was valuable in each source, and then distilling that information into key insights for the reader.

And now, I will offer one reason I did not write the books. I did not intend to write a scientific study, and these books are not academic endeavors; they do not have insights that can be tested through a scientific approach. The books were written to offer practical insights I felt were important to remember, with a particular emphasis on insights that could be used to improve the quality or success of life in the modern world. The insights are provided after a long and thoughtful process: reading hundreds of books and other sources across a range of fields, documenting the key insights from more than 150 of them, and trying to learn from them so they might be applied in life. The sources reflect my interests and do not even closely represent all of life's diverse subject matter. Heck, if I covered everything, then my readers would have nothing left to discover on their own!

Finally, I offer a brief commentary on the information referenced in the books. The information comes almost exclusively from its 150+ sources. My contribution has been to recognize what I believe are the sources' valuable insights, organize the sources into recognizable themes so the information flows as coherently as possible, and present the insights as concisely as possible. A full reference to each source is provided on the page of each source's key insights. Information directly attributed from a source is provided in quotations, and information not provided in quotations is either a paraphrase or my interpretation of that source's information. Providing each source's reference on the page of its key insights is also my way of encouraging readers to read some of the sources in their entirety.

I hope you enjoy the book!

CHAPTER 1:
SCIENCE, TECHNOLOGY,
AND SCIENCE FICTION

"Science is organized knowledge. Wisdom is organized life."

—Immanuel Kant

Idea Man: A Memoir by the Cofounder of Microsoft
by Paul Allen
(New York: Penguin Books, 2011)

Key Insights:

1. *Setting the Stage for the Future.* "My really big ideas have all begun with a stage-setting development . . . I ask a few basic questions: Where is the leading edge of discovery headed? What *should* exist but doesn't yet? How can I create something to help meet the need, and who might be enlisted to join the crusade? Whenever I've had a moment of insight, it has come from combining two or more elements to galvanize a new technology and bring breakthrough applications to a potentially new audience."

1

products so the consumer only sees how easy they are to use. Apple cares about the smallest detail, because each detail adds up to make something either easier or harder to use.

7. *Apple Is Expensive*. Apple will never compete on price, because Jobs says price competition is a race to the bottom that no one wins. Apple wins on quality, which is why it enjoys a 25% profit margin.

8. *Key People Make the Difference*. Jobs recruits the most talented people he can find. He believes there is not much difference in certain jobs, such as a cook or driver, but there is hundreds of times more impact in an excellent versus an average programmer.

9. *No Product Focus Groups, No Committees*. Apple does not systemize innovation. Jobs himself finds the next product gem out of hundreds of options. He does not trust consumers or employee committees to tell him where products, consumer demand, and the future will align. People cannot express what they want until it is created for them.

"The Decade of Steve (Jobs): His Legacy" by Adam Lashinsky (*Fortune*, November 23, 2009)

<u>Key Insights</u>:

1. *The Jobs Vision*. Steve Jobs is out to liberate the world through a peaceful revolution driven by his products. He thinks his products will help us be better humans. The key to the revolution is the fact that computing advances now allow individuals to do what only large groups could previously.

2. *The Jobs Persona.* Jobs is compelled by "intense drive, unflagging curiosity, and keen commercial imagination that have allowed (him) to see products and industries and possibilities that might be." He is an extremely hard worker and demanding of others. His actions are rapid fire, and they always aim to answer the question, "What is next?" Like Andrew Carnegie, he is extremely hands-on. Unlike Carnegie, Bill Gates, or other former industry giants, Jobs has not diverged from his core business—his revolution is his product.

3. *No Customer Surveys.* Much like Henry Ford, Jobs does not ask the customer what he wants, or he would end up with the computer-equivalent of a faster horse instead of a car. Jobs uses his own judgment to determine where customer desire is headed and then offers something totally new that is adopted in great numbers to meet that desire. Jobs is a one-man research and development machine, who says of his process, "there is a certain amount of homework involved . . . but mostly it's just picking up on things you can see on the periphery. Sometimes when you're almost asleep, you realize something you wouldn't otherwise have noted. I subscribe to a half-dozen Internet services, and I get about 300 emails a day, many from people I don't know, hawking crazy ideas. And I've always paid close attention to the whispers around me."

4. *Public Relations.* Jobs is famous for his new product launches, and he spends a huge amount of time scripting and preparing for them.

5. *Art and Science.* Gustave Eiffel was a brilliant architect because he was an engineer with an artistic touch, characteristics not commonly found in one person.

6. *Apple's Retail Touch.* Customers in Apple stores have no idea that immense amounts of research went into the store lighting to make Apple products as colorful as they appear in advertisements. Jobs does not need customers to know how much time was spent on the details; he simply wants them to "feel" the difference when they walk into an Apple store versus any other.

Newton
by Peter Ackroyd
(New York: Doubleday, 2006)

<u>Key Insights</u>:

1. *Abandonment = Success?* "It is often said that brilliant mathematicians tend to have solitary childhoods, in which they can explore the visionary world of numbers." Isaac Newton qualified in that regard. He was left by his mother to be cared for by his grandmother because the mother had remarried and the new husband did not want children.

2. *Early Characteristics.* The young Newton was inventive, preferring to tinker and build things rather than play with other children. He was an artisan as well as a calculator, loving both the arts and sciences. Like many geniuses who "cannot rely on the precepts of the masters," Newton preferred to learn on his own. He compiled notebooks on his reading and other interests, he organized and systematized his scattered areas of knowledge, and he set a goal of discovering solutions to 12 problems he wanted to solve within a year.

3. *Single-Mindedness.* Newton was single-minded in his focus on work to the point of obsession. He was so

focused that he did not pay much heed to life's routines, stayed up very late pursuing his breakthroughs, and sometimes forgot to eat. "His mental endurance, his ability to keep a problem in his mind for days or months on end, is probably without parallel." "He devoted all of his attention to a problem until he had satisfactorily resolved it; then he would abandon his work for a while. After a few months he would return to it, and make another leap forward. He learned how to "husband" his mind ... to allow it to lie fallow before it became fruitful once more."

4. *University Education.* Post-secondary education was loose in Newton's day; the curriculum was wide open and students slacked off. The advantage for the focused Newton was that he was free to study what interested him. "Newton hardly bothered with the ordinary curriculum, and at the last minute 'crammed' the orthodox textbooks so that he could at least pass each test in turn. His mind and imagination were elsewhere."

5. *Empiricism.* In the heart of the romantic age, Newton kicked off empirical science—the idea that theories must withstand observation through experimentation.

6. *Science and Religion* ... were one in the same to Newton in that he thought theology and science were equal avenues to God. He was in search of eternal truths through his scientific pursuits.

7. *Secrecy.* Newton kept his work to himself and published certain findings only if he saw others approaching his breakthroughs. He hated to be challenged intellectually on his work to the point he would rather not publish than get into disputes. He was not a good teacher and held tenure only to continue his research.

8. *Picturing Solutions.* Some wrote of Newton that he could "sometimes see almost by intuition, even without demonstration."

9. *Later Life.* Like many mathematicians and scientists, Newton knew his discoveries were over when he turned 40 years old. The last years of his life were spent running England's mint as its administrator. He also devoted significant time to revising and extending his legacy by releasing second and third editions of his old books.

The Field: The Quest for the Secret Force of the Universe
by Lynne McTaggert
(London: HarperCollins, 2001)

Key Insights:

1. *The Field Defined.* The field is a pulsating life force that we can connect to if we know how. It cuts across space and time, and it connects all ideas, minds, and thoughts.

2. *On Definitive Proof.* "A right idea can never get definitively proven." You can only disprove a wrong idea.

3. *We Are All Connected.* At a quantum level, the field represents an interconnection among all things that runs diametrically opposed to Darwinian evolution, which posits that things are in competition with one another. We live in community, we influence that community, and it influences us.

4. *The Force of Will.* Much of life remains undetermined until you will it into a direction, which is why the force of one's will is so powerful.

5. *The Field Taking Shape.* The field may be responsible for the structure of our bodies; it provides an unseen energy field around a child that covers his space that he will occupy as an adult.
6. *Consciousness* . . . is not housed in any one part of the brain; it is a field within the brain.
7. *Free Will* . . . could be the manifestation of our brains making quantum-level choices to take potential states of being into actual states from a variety of different options.
8. *Be Positive.* A positive outlook can change so much of your life in ways we do not even begin to understand.
9. *Where Will We End Up?* "To be a true explorer is to carry on exploration even if it takes you to a place you didn't particularly plan to go."

The Making of Second Life
by Wagner James Au
(New York: Collins, 2008)

Key Insights:

1. *Unlimited Virtual Reality.* According to Second Life founder, Philip Rosedale, "Somebody . . . will take the virtual worlds concept and expand it to its full potential, and that's going to be as large and as important as the personal computer or the web." Rosedale believes, "the leading edge of human evolution is culture and mind, and the trailing edge . . . is our bodies. In the future . . . (our) grandchildren will perceive the real world as a kind of 'museum or theater,' with realms like Second Life the locus for work and much of our personal relationships. In some sense, I think we will see the entire physical

world as being kind of left behind, and it will have this charming quality to us, like Williamsburg ...

2. *The Pace of Change.* "The physical world is evolving at exactly zero; the laws of physics are not changing. The simulation granularity and realism and fidelity of Second Life is increasing at Moore's Law; or beyond it, given some software work on top of it."

3. *Growing Fantasies.* Gartner, Inc. has predicted that 80 percent of all Internet uses will have a "second life" on the Internet. Over 90 percent of all South Koreans under the age of 30 have a cyber world account.

4. *Noosphere*—described in the early twentieth century by Jesuit priest, Father Pierre Teilhard de Chardin as "an aggregate of all human intellect, united electronically into a global mind."

5. *Social Downsides of Massively Multiuser Online (MMO) Worlds.* A Stanford University study found 50 percent of respondents described themselves as addicted to their MMO.

6. *Early Visions.* As a kindergartener, Philip Rosedale recalls thinking, "Why am I here, and how am I different from everybody else? What am I here to do? I always had this strong sense of 'I want to change the world somehow.'" Rosedale thinks he founded Second Life as a goal that would match that early vision.

7. *Death by Cash.* "Sometimes companies starve for lack of money, but sometimes they choke to death from too much."

8. *What People Do in Their Second Lives.* Given the opportunity to fly, perform amazing stunts, or otherworldly feats, people mostly choose to build homes, walk, and meet other people. They choose a simulated reality close to the one in their physical reality.

9. *A Theory of Justice.* In 1971, John Rawls posed a hypothetical assumption that if you did not know if you would be born smart or dull, you would willingly agree to a certain type of social contract that would offer protections for the least among us.

10. *Evolving Second Life.* "We figured if this was going to be like the world, we needed to speed up the evolutionary cycle . . . to compress two million years of human evolution into about five. If you have a genetic mutation that is better suited to the environment . . . it'll replicate really quickly."

The Singularity Is Near: When Humans Transcend Biology by Ray Kurzweil (New York: Viking, 2005)

Key Insights:

1. *Life's Overall Purpose* . . . is to move towards greater intelligence and knowledge.

2. *The Inventor's Rush.* In 1896, the inventor of alternating electrical current, Nikola Tesla said, "I don't think there is any thrill that can go through the human heart like that felt by the inventor as he sees some creation of the brain unfolding to success."

3. *On Catching the Inventor's Wave.* Most inventions fail because the timing is wrong. "Inventing is a lot like surfing; you have to anticipate and catch the wave at just the right moment."

4. *The Law of Accelerating Returns* . . . explains why technological and evolutionary processes progress in an exponential instead of linear fashion. Exponential growth curves start slow and then explode with

unexpected fury. Intuitively, it may not feel like huge progress, because in the short term, the exponential curve can fell like a straight line. Ray Kurzweil thinks humans are at the base of an exponential curve's explosion in information technology. He states, for example, that 99% of computing power is not being used, and that we will get a huge productivity boost when we tie all computers together into one network. He believes we will make 20 years of progress in 14 years, then we will do the same in the next seven years, and on and on until the 21st Century will produce 1,000 times greater progress than did the 20th Century.

5. *Why Will Technology Expand Exponentially?* Evolution is basically a runaway phenomenon. Through positive feedback loops that reward changes and choices that are successful, evolution creates a capability and then uses that capability to create the next stage of growth. For example, chemistry led to biology, which led to the human brain, which led to development of technology, which led to artificial intelligence, which will lead to the awakening of an intelligent universe.

6. *Punctuated Equilibrium* . . . is a concept in evolution characterized by periods of rapid changes followed by periods of stability whereby the changes are digested into the system as they are improved and refined prior to launching the next round of great changes.

7. *Single Trends* . . . cannot be forecasted forever into the future because other dynamics constantly intercede.

8. *Is the World a Computer?* Kurzweil says the world is an information network comprised of bits of data, not particles and forces. He wonders if the world is a giant computer being used by someone to solve a problem.

9. *On Deflation.* Deflation is being caused by global productivity increases and may not be the problem economists think it is. The technology sector deflates 40-50% annually, yet revenues grow 17% annually because more people are buying technology as it gets more powerful, user-friendly, and inexpensive.

10. *Technology's Adoption Rate.* Today, the delay between early and late adoption of new technology is 10 years, but by 2020, the lag time will be cut to five years.

11. *Information Civilizations.* A Type 2 Civilization has harnessed the power of its star for communications through electromagnetic radiation, which Kurzweil estimates of our civilization to occur in 2200. A Type 3 Civilization harnesses its entire galaxy for communications.

12. *On Scientific Revolutions.* Stephen Jay Gould said that the most important scientific revolutions dethroned human arrogance about our centrality in the cosmos.

13. *The March of Democracy.* The world has moved from 20 to 100 different democracies.

14. *Knowledge at Your Fingertips.* In 20 minutes online, you can now conduct the same research that used to take half of a day at the library.

15. *Change Is Hard.* "The human mind likes a strange idea as little as the body likes a strange protein and resists it with a similar energy."

Final Theory
by Mark Alpert
(New York: Touchstone, 2008)

<u>Key Insights</u>:

1. *Fight with What You Got.* "No time for second guessing . . . You go to war with the army you have."
2. *On Scrappiness.* "His father taught him the fundamental rule: Don't be afraid to fight dirty."
3. *Developing Scientific Theory.* You do not have to know all of the details to construct a general theory, just as Albert Einstein did not know all of the details behind his theories, some of which were discovered after his death. One researcher described the development of a general theory as, "more like a crossword puzzle than a jigsaw. As long as you have enough clues, you can figure out the pattern, and then you can fill in the blank spaces later."
4. *Einstein the Optimist.* "Einstein was a hopeless optimist. He really thought that in a few years the Americans and Russians would lay down their arms and form a world government. Then war would be outlawed and everyone would be at peace."

Cell
by Stephen King
(New York: Pocket Books, 2006)

<u>Key Insights</u>:

1. *Putting Losses Behind You.* "(She) had an advantage. She had suffered her losses and begun to move on."

2. *Find the Patterns.* The world is full of stories. If you can listen to enough of them, they can line up and make patterns.

3. *Risk Is Unavoidable.* "Little knowledge is gained without risk."

4. *Other Aspects of Evolution.* "What Darwin was too polite to say . . . is that we came to rule the earth not because we were the smartest, or even the meanest, but because we have always been the craziest, most murderous . . . in the jungle. Man has come to dominate the planet thanks to two essential traits. One is intelligence. The other has been the absolute willingness to kill anyone and anything that gets in his way."

5. *Intelligence Evolves.* "Mankind's intelligence finally trumped mankind's killer instinct, and reason came to rule over mankind's maddest impulses. That too was survival." If intelligence and reason did not win out, humans would have just killed each other forever.

6. *One Man's Terrorist Is Another Man's Freedom Fighter.* "When does a collaborator stop being a collaborator . . . When the collaborators become the clear majority . . . if you were a romantic, you called those people 'the underground.' If you weren't a romantic, you called them fugitives. Or maybe, just criminals."

7. *Identifying Extinction.* Extinction can be hard to spot. Some extinctions can be a slow decline over many years with a sudden drop-off at the end. The signs are there but maybe you did not know how to look for them.

CHAPTER 2:
LEADERSHIP, MANAGEMENT, AND ORGANIZATIONS

"When you grow up and have a job, do something you love. Whatever you do, you should love it."

—Advice given to Microsoft co-founder, Paul Allen by his father.

Business Stripped Bare
by Richard Branson
(London: Virgin Books, 2008)

Key Insights:

1. *Focus on Your Strengths*. Do not let your weaknesses and limitations get in the way of success. Focus on what you do well and leverage those abilities.
2. *Branson's Risks*. Richard Branson is a risk taker, but he always calculates his risks to ensure the odds are in his favor. He also diversifies his risks so that no single venture will bring his entire company down. As a risk taker, Branson loves the quote, "The brave may not live forever, but the cautious do not live at all."

3. *Investment Timing.* If he could live over again, Branson says he would only invest in recessions, when everything is selling for 50-90 percent of its intrinsic worth.

4. *Think Big, Build Small.* Branson believes in the entrepreneurial spirit of small enterprises, so his umbrella company has over 300 small companies within it, each trying to do its own job of growing. He takes good deputy managers, splits a company in half, and then allows each deputy to grow the new enterprises on their own. People get the opportunity to grow and expand both themselves and their companies at the same time.

5. *Oil Shock.* Branson believes the price of fuel will skyrocket due to human population demands on a limited world oil supply.

6. *Creative Business.* Branson is interested in creating things, and he believes business can be as creative as painting; it is risky and you do not want to ruin your canvas, but it is also inspiring.

7. *People Matter.* Branson believes, "business has to give people enriching, rewarding lives, or it's simply not worth doing."

8. *Merger Madness.* Branson believes business cultures are hard to merge. It is easier to start from scratch and build a new business that starts with your values at heart.

9. *Teamwork.* Albert Einstein said, "What a person does on his own, without being stimulated by the thoughts and experiences of others, is even in the best cases rather paltry and monotonous." Teams do not last forever, though, and Branson believes each team needs some combination of new and old blood to make them work.

10. *Don't Skimp on Capital.* Invest in the best equipment or you will live to regret it.

11. *The Heart of an Entrepreneur.* "Pragmatism over idealism, adventurers over fatalists, and optimists who can handle many different futures simply for the joy of doing so."

Up in the Air
by Walter Kirn
(New York: Doubleday, 2001)

<u>Key Insights</u>:

1. *Plans Gone Awry.* Always build a fudge factor for uncertainty into your plans.
2. *Gambling Addicts* . . . forget their losers when they hit a winner.
3. *Do I Go Out or Stay In?* People are in a constant search for the balance between linking with others and the desire to be by themselves.
4. *No Apologies.* To apologize for your core beliefs is to apologize for your very existence, so do not apologize for what you believe.
5. *Getting Taken.* At approximately 28 years old, after you have achieved a little success, you realize that you have been conned by some company that profits from your output.
6. *On Priorities.* "A man who confuses his business with his family risks losing both."
7. *Management Fallacy.* "In management, it's the stimulating assertion, not the tested hypothesis, that grabs folks."
8. *Winning and Keeping Customers.* Price discounting can work for a while by winning new customers, but it is better to be good than cheap. Cheap brings business; good brings loyalty.

9. *Hubris* . . . is when famous gurus pontificate on subjects about which they know little.

The Checklist Manifesto: How to Get Things Right
by Atul Gawande
(New York: Metropolitan Books, 2009)

Key Insights:

1. *Why Checklists Are Important.* Checklists do not help us with what we do not know; rather, they help us correctly apply what we already know. They also catch our human tendencies toward taking risks, craving adventure, and making decisions based on emotions versus facts. They are boring, routine, and mundane, but following a step-wise process over time leads to superior performance. Good checklists also leave room for judgment and intuition.

2. *On Productivity.* When you make many decisions, even correcting 1-2 percent of them leads to a big increase in productivity.

3. *Characteristics of a Good Checklist.* The good checklist is simple, to the point, and not too long. Typically, 5-10 items are a good length.

4. *Teams and Checklists.* Teams with checklists submit to a process instead of a strong leader or dogma that may or may not be correct.

5. *Know Someone's Name.* Being able to call someone by name is a proven way to be able to work better with him or her.

6. *A Famous Investor* . . . reads broadly and allows ideas to bubble through his brain. But when it comes time to invest, he submits his ideas to a detailed checklist for

every investment, and those that do not make it through the checklist do not get funded. He says this process a check on his "cocaine brain."

What Would Google Do? by Jeff Jarvis (New York: Collins Business, 2009)

Key Insights:

1. *Turn Enemies into Friends.* A company knows it has a problem if there is a big online following for a complainer's cause. Dell used its blog complainers to understand its problems and how to fix them. It turned its biggest complainers into people who helped it solve its problems—for free. Turning over control to the public can hurt a company's public relations in the short-term, but in the long-term, the company gets excellent feedback, solutions on how to fix problems, and a huge group of advocates.

2. *Network Theory*—a network is greater than the sum of its machines. One fax machine or computer is nothing unless connected with others around the world.

3. *Google's Fundamental Principle*—"It's best to do one thing really, really well."

4. *Middlemen Beware.* The Internet is eliminating the need for any person or industry that exists to sit between a buyer and a seller.

5. *Characteristics of the Evolving Online Universe*—transparency, honesty, collaboration, and simplicity. In an age of transparency, whereby nothing will be private, we must all be willing to forgive shortcomings

and transgressions that we are sure to discover of one another.

6. *Success in a Digital Universe.* The public, not institutions or high priests, will determine future success and failure. The reward for success will be *attention*.

7. *The Firm Is Dead?* Some claim that people will no longer be affiliated with organizations—that we will simply form and disperse around issues that bring us together based on our needs and interests.

8. *Google Time.* Google gives each employee 20 percent free time to work on projects of personal interest that can improve the company. This time is measured and outcomes are watched, but it allows employees the freedom to pursue passionate interests. The free time recommits the employees to Google, helps Google find new opportunities, and provides solutions to problems.

Confidence: How Winning Streaks and Losing Streaks Begin and End by Rosabeth Moss Kanter (New York: Three Rivers Press, 2004)

Key Insights:

1. *Boom or Bust.* "Sometimes it seems as if there are only two states of being: boom or bust. When things are up, it feels as if they will always be up. People come to believe they can succeed at anything they try . . . When things are down, it seems as if they will always be down . . . What causes them to rise or fall is often a matter of confidence." "On the way up, success creates positive momentum. People who believe they are likely to win are also likely to put in the extra effort at difficult moments

to ensure that victory. On the way down, failure feeds on itself." "Winning makes it easier to attract the best talent ... the biggest revenues to reinvest in perpetuating victory."

2. *Confidence* . . . "determines whether our steps . . . are tiny and tentative or big and bold." "Expectations about the likelihood of success determine the amount of effort people are willing to put in." "People who believe in themselves are likely to try harder and longer, thus increasing their chances of eventual success." "Confidence is the sweet spot between arrogance and despair ... Overconfidence leads people to overshoot ... underconfidence . . . leads people to underinvest, to under-innovate, and to assume that everything is stacked against them, so there's no point in trying."

3. *Patterns of Failure and Success.* "Failures and success are not episodes, they are trajectories. They are tendencies, directions, pathways ... the next performance is shaped by what happened last time out, unless something breaks the streak. The meaning of any particular event is shaped by what's come before. The same $10,000 in someone's bank account can make him feel rich and getting richer if he had only $5,000 the day before and $1,000 the day before that, or poor and getting poorer if he had $50,000 the previous day and $100,000 two days earlier. History and context shape interpretations and expectations."

4. *Perceptions.* Everything you do sends a message about being a winner or loser. Target, for example, won a major deal two years prior to Kmart's demise. Target's headquarters was crisper, its people were more alert and willing to make a deal to get new business.

5. *Relax Under Pressure.* Winning teams practice relaxing under pressure, because if they are too uptight or anxious, they will make mistakes. Winners and losers both make mistakes, but it is the loser's response—panic—that turns a small mistake into a losing situation.

6. *Confidence Cultures.* "Leaders (can create) a foundation for confidence that permits unexpected people to achieve high levels of performance, and to do it as part of a successful team. Each time the team or organization wins a victory, support for confidence is increased. An occasional win turns into a long winning streak." Leading organizations also do not count on impulse or mood to succeed; instead, they establish disciplines and processes to embed confidence in formal structures.

7. *The Pygmalion Effect.* "If teachers think students are in the top group (even if they were put there randomly), and thus treat them like high achievers, their performance improves—a self-fulfilling prophecy . . . Thinking that someone is a potential high performer encourages leaders and colleagues to look more closely at her, to invest more time, to pass on more tips, to find the positives that surely must be there and mention them, ignoring the negatives because surely they cannot be true."

8. *Emotional Contagion*—"The unconscious tendency to mimic another person's facial expressions, tone of voice, posture, and movements, even when one is focused on other things and is seemingly unaware of the model for the mood."

Michael J. Hillyard

The 100 Best Business Books of All-Time
by Jack Covert and Todd Satterstein
(New York: The Penguin Group, 2009)

Key Insights:

1. *Flow.* "Happiness comes in those moments of effortless
    concentration when minutes, even hours seem to pass
    without so much as a glance at the clock . . . when we
    are totally focused and un-selfconscious." This situation
    occurs when (a) our skills are adequate to cope with the
    challenge at hand, (b) we are in a rules-bound system
    with clear indications of how we are performing, and
    (c) we enjoy what we are doing. Games function in
    the broadest sense along these lines, so work should be
    structured as much like a game as possible. When the
    game loses its challenge and becomes rote, it is time to
    change the game.
2. *Getting Things Done.* The human brain continues to
    remind us of things when we cannot do anything about
    them. By using calendars and lists that we can review
    on a regular schedule, we not only make better progress
    towards things that are important, but we also set our
    mind at ease from having to continuously remind us of
    things we cannot immediately control.
3. *The Effective Executive.*
    a. Peter Drucker says to leverage our strengths
        and not focus on our weaknesses because our
        contribution is really the only measure of
        success. Contributions result from applying our
        strengths.

    b.   Drucker says to drop all unproductive behaviors and historical programs if they are not relevant in the future.

    c.   Simple solutions are the best solutions.

    d.   Three time sponges to avoid:

        i.   Doing things that do not need to be done.

        ii.   Doing things better done by others.

        iii. Doing things that force others to do unnecessary things.

4. *The 7 Habits of Highly Effective People.* The major themes of successful people are:

    a.   Character—integrity, industry, honesty, humility, simplicity.

    b.   Self-Mastery—personal control and discipline.

    c.   Cooperation—relationships grow through trust.

    d.   4 Dimensional Control—successful people feed their physical, mental, spiritual, and social/emotional needs.

5. *How to Win Friends and Influence People.* Ultimately, life comes down to relationships. One of the best things you can do in life is to make someone else feel important . . . and really mean it. It is the person not interested in his fellow man who provides the greatest injury to others.

6. *Swim with the Sharks.* If you meet a famous person, avoid the fan syndrome and talk to them about their interests.

7. *The Power of Intuition.* 90% of professionals use their intuition to make decisions.

8. *Oh, the Places You'll Go.* Life can be confusing, lonely, and dull, and getting through those periods is part of life's great journey.

9. *The Little Prince.* Life is futile if it lacks purpose.

10. *Chasing Daylight.* Embrace the time with family, friends, and ourselves because life can be short. You will never regret having spent that time.

11. *Leadership Is . . .*
    a. Defining the future and going there . . .
    b. Figuring out what you are good at and doing it . . .
    c. Not easy and requires daily attention and facing your fears . . .
    d. Best when the voice is strategic, persuasive, and tied to tangible results.

12. *Control Your Destiny or Someone Else Will.* A good business avoids slugfests with competitors and focuses on niches it can dominate. Jack Welch's standard was, "If you're not already in this business, would you enter it today?"

13. *Good to Great.* A good life mission can answer the following three questions: what can you be best in the world doing, what drives your economic engine, and what are you deeply passionate about?

14. *The Innovator's Dilemma.* The launch point for a disruptive innovation is usually too small for a large organization to see, which is why new and small organizations tend to produce the next big thing.

15. *Who Says Elephants Can't Dance.* "Big matters. Size can be leveraged. Breadth and depth allow for greater investment, greater risk taking, and longer patience for payoffs."

16. *Positioning.* If you cannot be first in a category, start a new category because no one remembers second place, the second guy to break a record, or the second market share position. Today's world is so cluttered, you need

the equivalent position of "Volvo = Car Safety" or "Costco = Cheap Bulk Goods."

17. *Lucky or Smart?*
    a. Entrepreneurs are luckier than is traditionally acknowledged as to why they have been successful.
    b. Businesses, cities, industries, or even people can get an edge by being perceived as hip, cool, and smart by the talented people they are trying to attract.

18. *Beyond the Core.* Only 25% of growth investments add value, and most growth investments fail. New products fail 70% of the time, startup companies fail 95% of the time, joint ventures fail 80% of the time, and acquisitions fail 70% of the time.

19. *The Best Business Proverb of All-Time.* "A bird in hand is worth two in the bush."

20. *Driven.* There are four fundamental human evolutionary traits: acquire, bond, learn, and defend. Do not let one of these traits control you at the expense of the others.

CHAPTER 3:
ECONOMICS, FINANCE,
AND INVESTING

"Programs, organizations, and systems work better
when they get the incentives right. It is like rowing
downstream."

—Charles Wheelan

Aftershock: The Next Economy and America's Failure
by Robert Reich
(New York: Vintage Books, 2010)

Key Insights:

1. *Entrepreneurial Climate.* Entrepreneurial activities jump in prosperous times, "when the purchasing power of the masses increases their demands for a higher standard of living and enables them to purchase more than their bare wants."
2. *Wealthy Isolation.* "Being rich now means having enough money that you don't have to encounter anyone who isn't."

3. *On Capitalism's Shortfall.* John Maynard Keynes said capitalism, on its own without government direction, cannot provide full employment and it creates an inequitable distribution of wealth. When wealth is too narrowly concentrated at the top, overall demand shrinks because the wealthy do not spend everything they earn. The middle class spends a higher percentage of their net worth.

4. *Keeping up with the Joneses.* Social comparisons influence people in different ways. They try to keep pace with those who are economically ahead of them. And, when people lose something, they feel worse than if they never had it at all.

The Money Makers: How Extraordinary Managers Win in a World Turned Upside Down
by Anne-Marie Fink
(New York: Crown Business, 2009)

Key Insights:

1. Knowledge... is the highest return asset in any business.
2. *"Economics Trumps Management."* Warren Buffett said, "When a good manager joins a bad business, the latter usually retains its reputation."
3. *"Good Performance Requires Inefficiency and Duplication."* If taken too far, a quest for efficiency drives out new ideas, creativity, and innovation, especially in areas of research and development.
4. *Comfort Is the Enemy of Success.* A company with a happy workforce does not necessarily mean it is a good one in which to invest. Some of the best investments are in

companies that drive people hard and consistently push them to levels most people would find uncomfortable.

5. *Small Steps Beat Bold Transformations.* Successful companies take small steps in the right direction to improve. Bold transformations are not nearly as common in building great companies.

6. *The Shrinking Company.* "Not all growth is good. Revenue and income growth that use more resources than they generate do not advance economic profit and do not create value." Shrinking a company out of areas that do not cover their cost of capital and then reinvesting in stronger areas can be a good way to shrink a company to longer-term success.

7. *"Investors Spend a Lot of Time Being Wrong."* At best, professional investors are right 60% of the time. When wrong, they cut their losses quickly and move on.

8. *All Technologies Eventually Become Commodities.* "Most companies are "unprepared when their core products no longer earn superior returns."

9. *The Cockroach Theory.* Some investors sell an investment at the first sign of trouble, because problems are like cockroaches—there is always more than one.

10. *A Tight Ship.* "Running tight on capital forces astute decision making."

11. *Don't Always Listen to the Customer.* Many successful companies rely much more on their own insights than those of their customers because customers do not have see the big picture when they offer recommendations, problems, or solutions.

12. *Risk Ignorance.* "Many executives underestimate the risks they take that produce the rewards they enjoy."

13. *Economic Forecasts Are Largely Bunk.* Prepare for many different alternative futures when considering your business strategies.
14. *Duration Risk.* "The more time between investment and payback, the greater the risk." Successful companies focus on projects with quick paybacks. Making bets on projects with far-off cash flows invite steep odds.
15. *Balancing Risk.* "Two types of risk exist—the risk of going out on a limb and the risk of holing up in a safe place—and success comes from balancing between the two."

Getting Back to Even
by James J. Cramer with Cliff Mason
(New York: Simon and Schuster, 2009)

Key Insights:

1. *Visual Reminders.* Jim Cramer still keeps a copy of his hedge fund's lowest portfolio value in his wallet to remind him of how scary things can get.
2. *Buy and Hold Is Bunk.* Cramer says buying and holding is the worst conventional investing wisdom ever offered.
3. *When Things Look Bad, Sell!* "When the outlook is terrible, your bias must be to sell." There is a 75% chance that your failed investment will never get back to even.
4. *The Best Companies* . . . possess things or processes that cannot be copied.
5. *During Bear Market Drops* . . . normal valuation metrics simply do not apply. It is as if the rules of the market have been suspended.

6. *Take Your Profits.* Cramer has to continuously remind himself to take profits off the table because "hogs get slaughtered."
7. *Diversify!* Cramer says that no more than 20 percent of your portfolio should be in a single sector.
8. *You Will Be Wrong.* Every investor is wrong at some point, and how you prepare for being wrong is as important as how you prepare for being right.
9. *Dividends Are Your Friend.* More than 40 percent of stock gains come from dividends. A 5 percent dividend yield doubles your money in 14 years even if the stock price stagnates. Earnings should be at least twice the dividend yield to cover any problems associated with paying the dividend or having it cut.
10. *Don't Predict the Future.* Good investors do not try to predict the future; they assess risk and probabilities associated with various futures and make their investment with the least risk and highest probability of success.

The Most Important Thing:
Uncommon Sense for the Thoughtful Investor
by Howard Marks
(New York: Columbia University Press, 2011)

Key Insights:

1. *There Is No Silver Bullet to Investing.* "Successful investing requires thoughtful attention to many separate aspects, all at the same time."
2. *The Number One Investing Principle.* Avoid big mistakes and avoidable errors. The goal as an investor is not to hit

great tennis shots; instead, it is to simply keep the ball in play by avoiding bad shots.

3. *Cycles Always Prevail in the End.* "Trees don't grow to the sky. Few things go to zero." "Success carries within itself the seeds of failure, and failure the seeds of success." "The worst loans are made in the best of times." "The air goes out of the balloon much faster than it went in." The best investors watch the herd swing from optimism and pessimism and then do the opposite from the herd when the market reaches extremes.

4. *Risk Versus Return.* Limiting risk is more important than trying to achieve a huge return. "Over a full career, most investor's results will be determined more by how many losers they have, and how bad they are, than by the greatness of their winners."

5. *Themes of the Great Investors*: (1) avoid human foibles, (2) be patient and contrarian, (3) have reasonable expectations, (4) measure probability and expected outcomes, (5) take conscious risk into consideration, and (6) make bets where you can make a lot but only lose a little.

6. *2nd Level Thinking is the Key to Investing.* You have to be able to see what others or the market cannot see about the future.

7. *Be Patient.* Do not expect the market to immediately recognize your insight. Securities can remain mispriced for a long time, and you may lose money before your insights are recognized in the market.

8. *On Risk and Returns.* "The safest and most potentially profitable thing is to buy something when no one else likes it." Most hugely profitable investments begin with discomfort because they cut against the grain of popular opinion. Making an investment in something that has

been shunned until it becomes merely tolerable can lead to huge gains. Risk can be greater in a boom than in a recession—prices have further to fall if something goes wrong.

9. *On Poor Investing Logic.* "People should like something less when its price rises, but in investing they often like it more."

10. *Avoidable Human Investing Flaws* . . . include the desire for more, missing out on others' gains, and comparing yourself to others.

11. *Oaktree's Investment Principles.* (1) Is there intrinsic value, (2) You must act when price diverges from intrinsic value, (3) When things are too good to be true . . . they are, and (4) Markets always move in cycles.

12. *Be Hunted, Not the Hunter.* If you wait for investments to come to you instead of chasing them, you will get a better price. The best prices come when someone is forced to sell.

13. *Predicting Markets Is Like Predicting the Weather.* Most macro economic forecasts are bunk.

Your Money and Your Life:
A Lifetime Approach to Money Management
by Robert Aliber
(Stanford, California: Stanford Economics and Finance, 2010)

Key Insights:

1. *An Investing Plan Is a Must.* Yogi Berra said, "If you don't know where you're going, you'll end up someplace else."

2. *There's No Escape from Inflation.* Severe U.S. inflation occurs almost once per generation. Be prepared for it, since the last serious bout of inflation occurred in the 1970's.

3. *Home Management Costs.* Annual home costs are approximately 3% of a home's market value. For example, if a home is worth $2 million, its annual home costs will run approximately $60,000.

4. *Not All Land Is Equal.* Not all land rises in value after inflation is considered. Lakes, rivers, oceans, and proximity to urban amenities tend to rise more rapidly than do other areas.

5. *Limit Theorem.* When prices of an asset rise rapidly, they will eventually fall to reflect the fact that nothing can remain above the level of household incomes' ability to pay for it. In a macro sense, U.S. corporate profits closely link to U.S. Gross Domestic Product growth (or decline)—profits will not just rise on their own without growth in the economy.

6. *Don't Be Illogical About Insurance.* "Americans spend too much money on nickel/dime losses" and not enough to protect against true catastrophes. "The risks that should be insured are those where the probable loss is large and could lead to a significant decline in your standard of living."

7. *Specialization Versus Diversification.* "Fortunes are made (and lost) by specialization; fortunes are conserved by diversification."

8. *Organizational Life Cycles.* A firm can be a real leader for 15-20 years, and although there are exceptions, eventually those "firms fall behind because they can't maintain their share of profits" in their industry. They get displaced by competitors or technology.

9. *5 Investor Mistakes*:
   a. Investors buy an asset without an exit strategy.
   b. Investors believe tomorrow will be like today.
   c. Investors hold out for the last dollar and "ignore the fact that when stock prices decline, they decline much more rapidly than they increase."
   d. When a portfolio rises, investors misattribute luck to skill and then boldly overreach in future investments.
   e. Investors ignore an investment loss if they hold onto a losing asset instead of selling it because they believe the loss is not real until it is recognized through a sale.

The Age of Turbulence: Adventures in a New World by Alan Greenspan (New York: Penguin Books, 2007)

Key Insights:

1. *Less Is More.* "In times of great national urgency, every congressman feels he has to put out a bill; presidents feel the pressure to act too. Under those conditions you can get counterproductive policies ..."
2. *Society's Core.* "Short of a few ambiguous incidents, I can think of no circumstances where the expanded rule of law and enhanced property rights failed to increase material prosperity."
3. *The Factors of Global Growth*:
   a. *Free Trade.* The extent of domestic competition and a country's openness to trade and international integration.

      b.   *Capable Institutions.* The quality of a country's institutions to make an economy work.

      c.   *Economic Stability.* Policymakers' ability to enact macroeconomic stability.

      d.   *Protection of Property Rights.* A country's ability to protect private property and ownership rights, which are the keys to self-interest and motivation.

4. *The Approval of Others.* "All people appear motivated by an inbred striving for self-esteem that is in large part fostered by the approval of others."

5. *On Ability.* Sometimes, when you see a great talent, you can envision yourself working hard and being able to rise to that level, but in other situations, you realize the talent comes from a genetic origin, and you know that you will never get to that level.

6. *Creative Destruction.* "A market economy will incessantly revitalize itself from within by scrapping old and failing businesses and then reallocating resources to newer, more productive ones."

7. *Aristotelian Ethics.* "Individuals have innate nobility and ... the highest duty of every individual is to flourish by realizing that potential."

8. *Compromise in a Democratic Republic.* "The existence of a democratic society governed by the rule of law implies a lack of unanimity on almost every aspect of the public agenda. Compromise on public issues is the price of civilization, not an abrogation of principle."

9. *On Overregulation.* "Deregulation was the Ford Administration's great unsung achievement. It's difficult to imagine how straightjacketed American business was then ... operations were monitored down to the tiniest detail."

10. *The Economy As a Large Vessel.* "Because a modern economy involves so many moving parts, it rarely accelerates or decelerates smoothly . . ."

11. *The Big Picture.* Ronald Reagan was always worried about being overbriefed. His emphasis was on the big picture.

12. *On Reform.* When a planned economy is broken, sometimes you just need to start over with a price system and shock the economy back to life. Small steps may not work.

13. *Historical Enemies of Private Property.* Communism was not the first condemnation of Capitalism. The notion that private property is sinful has deep roots in Christianity, Islam, and other religions.

14. *Limits of Prediction.* "You can't tell when a market is overvalued, and you can't fight market forces."

15. *Inflation.* In 2003, mortgages were below six percent for the first time since the 1960's.

16. *Unearned Wealth.* As seen in oil nations and inheritances, "easy, unearned wealth tends to dampen productivity."

17. *Adam Smith on Prosperity.* "Little else is required to carry a state to the highest degree of opulence . . . but peace, easy taxes, and a tolerable administration of justice: all the rest being brought about by the natural course of things."

18. *Capitalism's Outcomes.* Capitalism enhances the overall wealth of society, but it (a) does not treat all citizens the same, and (b) creates an inherent tension because it forces continued risk-taking, innovation, and destruction of companies that cannot keep up.

19. *Wealth Expectations.* "The cheer of new affluence rapidly fades and, with time, becomes the base from which additional, even higher, expectations evolve."

20. *John Maynard Keynes on Printing Money.* "There is no subtler, no surer means of overturning the existing basis of society than to debauch the currency. The process engages all the hidden forces of economic law on the side of destruction, and it does so in a manner which not one man in a million is able to diagnose."

21. *The Factors of Economic Growth: Population and Productivity.* Productivity will likely average two percent annually in the United States through 2030.

22. *Realizing the Gains from Invention.* It sometimes takes a long time for an invention to lead to productivity growth. For example, electronic power took a generation until it replaced steam power because of existing factories, households, and other steps in the power process that were already configured for steam.

23. *Inflation Will Strike When* . . . the supply of global cheap labor from formerly planned economies becomes more expensive as those economies rise. The long-term inflation rate will likely average 4.5 percent. Before 2030, we will likely see an 8 percent 10-year treasury bond yield.

The Rational Optimist: How Prosperity Evolves
by Matt Ridley
(New York: HarperCollins, 2010)

Key Insights:

1. *Financial Volatility.* Markets in capital and assets are much more volatile than markets in goods and services. Hiding or manipulating money is much easier than goods or services, which is why regulation in financial industries is much more critical than in goods and services.

2. *Two Key Underpinnings of Human Evolution*: (1) specialization (i.e., the division of labor), and (2) exchange (i.e., markets). Markets build trust; so much of their success depends on the faith people have in future deals.

3. *Misunderstanding the Past and Future.* Human progress marches forward, but we have a tendency to look back and see greatness and look forward and see doom. The odds are strongly in favor of our continuing to advance.

4. *A Definition of Prosperity.* "The increase in the amount of goods and services you can earn with the same amount of work." By this measure, health care and education are the only things that cost more now than they did in 1950.

5. *How to Make a Fortune.* Most fortunes are made making something less expensive than it previously was and then selling that improvement to the masses.

6. *Wanting Versus Being Thankful.* By nature, we are programmed to desire, not to appreciate.

7. *Observations of Evolution.* Cooking enabled humans to shrink their gut size and increase their brain. Digestion is easier with cooked food. Early humans were also able to diversity their food sources to avoid dependence on any single source and thus avoid starvation.

8. *One Way to Excellence* . . . is to copy the world's expert at the activity you want to master.

9. *On Group Dynamics.* The more cooperative a group is internally among its members, the more likely there will be hostility between groups.

10. *Turnover in Corporations.* Half of today's corporations did not exist in 1980. Innovation, since it comes from the economy's fringes and outliers, tends to favor new and small companies. In the past 25 years, the average company size has shrunken from 25 to 10 employees.

The Crash of '79
by Paul Erdman
(Berkeley, California: Berkeley Press, 1988)

Key Insights:

1. *Black Swan Risk.* Two huge banks named Franklin National and Herstatt went belly-up in 1974. Even billion dollar institutions can crumble.

2. *On Negotiations.* It never pays to negotiate on the other guy's home turf.

3. *The Big Picture.* A financier who was managing $300 billion for Saudi Arabia was asked why he was scrambling to save a $3 billion loss in the account. He then realized that his focus should be on much bigger issues.

4. *On Diversification.* Do not concentrate your deposits and investments in one country and currency.

5. *On Development.* To develop anything, you need two ingredients: capital and manpower. Saudi Arabia lacks manpower—the men do not work in manual labor jobs and the women do not work in the formal economy at all.

6. *Money Talks.* You can buy power and influence in the United States.

7. *Don't Be So Serious.* Nothing in your business or career should be taken too seriously; it all fades away with time.

8. *Why America Prospers.* America's magnet is not the Constitution or freedom—it is the chance to make a huge pile of money.

9. *Enjoy the Moment.* "Take the accolades when they come and relish them to the hilt, because when they stop . . . they are lost and gone forever."
10. *He Who Hesitates* . . . to act on information is lost.
11. *During an Economic Panic* . . . either sell before the panic or ride it all the way out. Those who lose the most are the ones who sell during the panic.

Scorecasting: The Hidden Influences Behind How Sports Are Played and Games Are Won
by Tobias Moscowitz and L. Jon Wertheim
(New York: Crown Archetype, 2011)

Key Insights:

1. *4 Psychological Insights*
    a. What is recognizable is often given too much credit versus what is concealed.
    b. Incentives are *very* powerful motivators, sometimes with undesirable consequences.
    c. Human biases play a role in every aspect of life.
    d. The role of luck is underappreciated and misunderstood.
2. *Active Versus Passive Mistakes.* People view acts of omission (inaction) as less harmful than acts of commission (action), but they should be viewed the same. For example, in most large corporations, "managers are obsessed with avoiding actual errors rather than missing opportunities." Also, "in the face of gain, we perform conservatively, more concerned about 'don't mess it up' defense than about 'gotta get it done' offense."
3. *On Winning and Losing.* "Losing hurts twice as bad as winning feels good." "Investors routinely sell winning

stocks too early and hold on to the dogs for too long." Do not let this irrational bias influence your behavior.

4. *Social Influences.* Two factors lead to hometown teams benefiting from a winning edge over visiting teams: (1) referees want to fit in with crowd expectations, and (2) referees think the crowd knows more than they do. Both of these biases are common subconscious psychologies.

5. *Overconfidence.* As a rule, people are overconfident in their abilities.

The Strategic Bond Investor: Strategies and Tools to Unlock the Power of the Bond Market by Anthony Crescenzi (New York: McGraw-Hill, 2010)

Key Insights:

1. *"Don't Fight the Fed."* The U.S. Federal Reserve Bank has enormous influence on the markets and the economy. The Fed has strong control over short-term interest rates, but it cannot control long-term rates. When the Fed raises rates, stocks will generally fall at some point. When the Fed lowers rates, stocks will generally rise at some point. As a rule of thumb, rising interest rates weaken the economy, and falling interest rates strengthen the economy. When the Fed raises rates, it is best to reduce exposure to economically sensitive investments and industries. Investors who show early confidence in the Fed's actions are likely to get better returns than those who do not, despite the fact that it can take years for the economy to change.

2. *Yield Curve Inversions.* When yields on investments in money markets, CD's, or other money instruments

pay more to invest short-term than long-term (which is an aberration), it is a general indication of coming economic problems.

3. *10-Year Treasury Yields.* The 10-Year Treasury Bond is a benchmark, and it usually yields between 2-4 percent, except in extraordinary times.

4. *Institutions and Bonds.* Institutions dominate the bond market. Any trade less than $1 million in the bond market is considered an "odd lot."

5. *Bond Portfolio Returns.* "The lionshare of the total return of a bond portfolio is ... driven by ... big picture, top-down variables." All of the other factors associated with bond purchases, such as negotiating a slightly better price when you purchase a bond, are merely marginal improvements. The big picture factors that influence bonds are interest rates, the economy, and the Fed.

6. *Bond Durations.* Short-term bonds extend from 1-5 years, mid-term bonds extend from 5-12 years, and long-term bonds extend from 12 years and beyond.

7. *Yield-to-Maturity.* The yield-to-maturity on a bond includes the hypothetical reinvestment of dividends at the yield-to-maturity rate. Interest on interest accounts for one-half of a bond's rate of return.

8. *Inflation.* If a bond pays 5 percent and inflation rises 5 percent, the bond's coupon payment has been completely negated by inflation.

9. *Irrationality.* Herd behavior can drive markets until one shock sends investor sentiment strongly in the opposite direction.

The Big Short: Inside the Doomsday Machine
by Michael Lewis
(New York: W. W. Norton and Company, 2010)

Key Insights:

1. *On the Outside Looking In.* Sometimes, it is the guy who is outside of the system who can see that the system is broken prior to the guy on the inside recognizing that anything is wrong. The investors who made money on the subprime mortgage crisis were oddballs who saw angles on the crisis from outside the system.

2. *Gutwrenching Investments.* There is nothing harder to do than to bet against the system. Your gut, your colleagues, the financial press, and the general public all subtly pressure you towards looking at things their way. You need to bet on what you really believe in order to make big profits.

3. *On Risk.* "Anything can happen to anyone at any time."

4. *On Commitment.* Warren Buffett said, "Writing a check separates a commitment from a conversation."

5. *Know Your Investing Style.* No school can teach you your unique investing style. You have to learn investing and find your niche in your own way. Even Warren Buffett applies value investing in his own way.

6. *Never Underestimate Incentives.* Warren Buffett's investing partner, Charlie Munger, says that incentives govern *everything*. You can predict how people will behave based on the incentives available to them.

7. *Be Patient.* Value investors sometimes have to wait years for the market to reward their low-priced stock.

8. *Change Your Mind.* Stay open-minded enough to change your mind on an investment at any time, and do not be stuck defending a bad investment decision.

How Markets Fail: The Logic of Economic Calamities
by John Cassidy
(New York: Farrar, Straus, and Giroux, 2009)

Key Insights:

1. *Market Failure Characteristics.* Market failures typically occur in non-production areas of the economy, such as insurance, technology, finance, and real estate. Leverage, efficiencies, and incentives in these systems are less transparent.

2. *Heuristics.* When faced with tough choices, we rely on shortcuts, we are influenced by others' opinions, and we tend to follow what others are doing.

3. *Herding* . . . occurs when everyone copies the same strategy and exhausts it until it collapses. We need to fight the urge to join the crowd in these situations, because the urge to follow a crowd actually has an evolutionary neurological basis.

4. *The Father of Capitalism.* Adam Smith was an ugly man who stammered when he spoke, and he also talked to himself in public. Smith grounded his theories in observation of reality, not abstract principles. Smith believed in only three roles for government: defense, justice, and public works.

5. *Non-Market Characteristics of Banking.* Smith did not include regulation as a government role in the economy, but he did note that banking was an area that required oversight because it did not naturally conform to market

forces. Hidden information is the biggest problem in financial systems, and government regulation is the only way to provide transparency.

6. *Life's Ultimate Struggle*. Smith believed much of life's struggle was a mental battle between instant gratification and long term planning.

7. *The Price System* . . . is the most efficient way to communicate information from consumer demand all the way through end inventory production.

8. *Calm Versus Stormy Markets*. Research has proven that markets go through calm periods where much new information does not move them and stormy periods where small changes create intense fluctuations.

9. *Uncertainty Is the Only Certainty*. John Maynard Keynes said that we cannot forecast anything very well over 10 or 20 years.

10. *Two Brains*. Our brain functions in two general ways. The first is when it is on autopilot, and our thinking and actions just sort of flow. The second is the conscious brain in which we think deliberately, follow specific rules, and act accordingly. The second approach is essential when making difficult decisions, such as investing.

***Financial Intelligence: A Manager's Guide to Knowing What the Numbers Really Mean*
by Karen Berman and Joe Knight with John Case
(Boston: Harvard Business School Press, 2006)**

Key Insights:

1. *Don't Trust the Numbers*. Accounting and finance are only a reflection of reality and can vary widely based on assumptions and estimates. Companies that are

reasonable and consistent with their financial reporting tend to have things work out in the long run. The most common source of accounting fraud is in the area of sales and revenues, and the fraud typically occurs in the company's timing of when it recognizes the revenues. Speeding up the recognition of revenues inflates a company's numbers in the short-term reporting period.

2. *Cash Is King.* Cash is the one issue in financial statements that is hard to fudge. Warren Buffett looks for cash-strong companies, because they have proven they know how to make money. Profits, on the other hand, are not real money because capital expenses do not count against profits and expenses are matched against revenues.

3. *Capital Expenses* . . . are expenses over a certain dollar amount.

4. *Have a Financial Plan.* Laurence Peter said, "If we don't know where we're going, we'll probably end up somewhere else."

5. *The Matching Principle.* Sales should be linked to their associated expenses.

6. *Depreciation* . . . is logged as an expense on the income statement only for the amount of depreciation incurred in the reporting period of the income statement.

7. *Operating Expenses.* Cutting expenses can produce short-term profitability, but the only ways to long-term growth are by increasing profitable sales and reducing expenses by becoming more efficient.

8. *Balance Sheet Misperceptions.* A company's balance sheet can be undervalued because assets are listed at their purchase price, not at what they could fetch on the open market. Land, for example, is usually undervalued on the balance sheet.

9. *Opposing Views on Employees.* Some companies view employees as assets into which they will invest, and other companies view employees as expenses to be used.

The House Advantage: Playing the Odds to Win Big in Business
by Jeffrey Ma
(New York: Palgrave MacMillan, 2010)

Key Insights:

1. *The Feeling of Losing a Fortune.* Ernest Hemmingway's character in *The Sun Also Rises* reflects on how he went bankrupt: "gradually, and then suddenly." Succumbing to risk can be a slow creep and then suddenly feel as though you fell off a cliff.

2. *Find Your Own "House Advantage."* Getting an edge can be as simple as following a disciplined success formula and sticking to it. Good analysis does not have to be perfect; it just has to be better than what everyone else is using. General George Patton said, "A good plan violently executed now is better than a perfect plan executed next week." You also have to be willing to recheck your strategy as the world changes. If you cannot find an edge, then do not bet.

3. *Be Able to Withstand Losses.* If you bet with the odds in your favor, you still need enough money to withstand the impact of short-term variances, because even with the odds in your favor, it is not uncommon to walk away a loser in the short-run. A good bet may lose 20 percent of the time. You have to be able to withstand short-term losses in order to reap long-term gains.

4. *Statistical Analysis.* Sometimes, math will tell you to do counterintuitive things in order to maximize your

opportunities. A human flaw is to notice data that supports our thesis and ignore data that does not. "People are twice as likely to seek out information that confirms their beliefs than they are to consider evidence that contradicts them."

5. *Positive Psychology.* You will never win over the long haul if you are a pessimist who questions your own success and wonders when it will end. You cannot be afraid to lose, and you have to have the courage to maximize the smart bet. The bigger the edge that you have, the larger the size of your bet should be.

6. *Action Versus Inaction.* Most people err on the side of inaction versus action. "Omission bias" is a human flaw that makes us feel better if we wait and see instead of taking action. You need to act when it is time to do so, even if it is uncomfortable. Not making a decision is the same as making one. Before making a decision, try to picture all possible outcomes, and when you have decided the best course of action based on those possible outcomes, then you need to act.

7. *Unconventional Thinkers Don't Win Popularity Contests.* John Maynard Keynes said unconventional thinkers can't win in the court of public opinion, because when they are right, the public thinks it is because of their rashness, and when they are wrong, the public says, "I told you so!"

SuperFreakonomics: Global Cooling, Patriotic Prostitutes, and Why Suicide Bombers Should Buy Life Insurance by **Steven Levitt and Stephen Dubner** **(New York: HarperLuxe, 2009)**

Key Insights:

1. *Incentivizing Human Ingenuity.* "When the solution to a given problem doesn't lay right before our eyes, it is easy to assume that no solution exists. But history has shown again and again that such assumptions are wrong." People respond to incentives, and incentives have unintended consequences. Selflessness will never solve big problems, such as global warming. Aligning incentives for people to think about society's most vexing problems solves them.

2. *Don't Drink and Drive.* A drunk driver is 13 times more likely to cause an accident than a sober one.

3. *No Matter Your Profession . . . Study Finance.* "All else being equal, there's a strong correlation between a finance background and career earnings."

4. *Cognitive Drift . . .* is what happens if more than one second elapses between clicking a mouse and seeing new data on the screen.

5. *It's Healthy on the Pedestal.* "Status seems to work a health-giving magic." For example, Nobel Prize winners live longer than do runners-up.

6. *Statistics Matter.* As the President of Ford Motor Company, Robert McNamara used statistics instead of emotions or politics to make his decisions. He introduced the seat belt based on statistical data that proved it could save lives.

7. *Focus on What You Can Change.* Focus on things you can change in life. "The Environment" is way too complex

for a human being to tackle. Direct your energies toward things you can impact.

Free: How Today's Smartest Businesses Profit by Giving Something for Nothing
by Chris Anderson
(New York: Hyperion, 2009)

Key Insights:

1. *Two Economies.* The atoms economy of tangible goods is inflationary; the digital economy is deflationary. The net annual deflation rate of the online economy is 50%, so it is 50% cheaper to deliver the same thing this year as it was last year.

2. *On Efficiencies and Growth.* Industrial processes improve their efficiency at a predictable 10-15 percent rate, with each doubling of volume due to what is called the "experience curve." Digital processes move much faster toward efficiency. The typical digital process has a familiar pattern: a new technology is introduced, the process to exploit that technology is honed, add-on technologies round out the exploitation, and the process is further honed until a new technology comes along when it is no longer cost efficient to continue sharpening the old process. Compound growth is created when efficiencies are realized at the same time new inventions or innovations are introduced into the system.

3. *Fundamental Versus Observational Knowledge.* If you understand the principles behind why something works, you get better productivity than if you only know anecdotally that something works.

4. *Social Networks.* In the physical world, 150 people are the maximum number of participants in a strong socially connected world. Online societies can retain their strength at much larger numbers of people.

5. *Outward Versus Inward Societies.* The social surpluses created in corn societies allowed those societies to be outward-focused traders and conquerors because the protein/labor ration in corn is so much higher than in rice or wheat. Japan and China have historically been inward-focused because rice is the most labor-intensive crop.

6. *Why Overpopulation Isn't a Problem.* The human race has been getting smarter at a faster pace than we have been reproducing. We extract resources from the earth faster than we can use them.

7. *Why Free Is Different.* Free is a unique price point because you consume without any mental decision-making. It is psychologically different than even paying one penny for a good or service. There are absolutely zero mental transaction costs associated with getting something for free. "The biggest gap in any venture is that between a service that is free and one that costs a penny."

Where Are All the Customers' Yachts?:
Or A Good Hard Look at Wall Street
by Fred Schwed
(New York: Simon and Schuster, 1940)

Key Insights:

1. *Financial Bubbles* . . . may have different industries from which they arise, but you need to get out when you see the standard characteristic common to all of them,

which is people not valuing money. To be a true investor, you have to be able to withstand watching young people who know nothing make huge profits for two, three, or four years before their crash. Sitting tight and being patient are hard for an investor, but sometimes they are the right things to do.

2. *The Best Investment Advice.* "When there is a stock market boom and everyone is scrambling for common stocks, take all your common stocks and sell them. Take the proceeds and buy conservative bonds. No doubt the stocks you sold will go higher. Pay no attention to this—just wait for the depression, which will come sooner or later. When this depression—or panic—becomes a national catastrophe, sell out the bonds (perhaps at a loss) and buy back the stocks. No doubt the stocks will go still lower. Again pay no attention. Wait for the next boom. Continue to repeat this operation as long as you live, and you'll have the pleasure of dying rich."

3. *American Humorists* . . . share "a passion for ideas, a keen sense of justice, and outrage that the world is the way it is instead of the way it should be."

4. *The Individual Investor* . . . "is still situated at the very bottom of the food chain, a speck of plankton afloat in a sea of predators." Most of the predators are not even good at what they do. "Thus far in our history there has been little evidence that there exists a demonstrable skill in managing security portfolios."

5. *You Are Not An Investor If* . . . you are not a skeptic, you obsess about a stock's price but know nothing of its business that it represents, you do not know who runs the company, or you do not know if it is profitable.

6. *Speculation Versus Investing.* "Speculation is an effort, probably unsuccessful, to turn a little money into a lot.

Investing is an effort, which should be successful, to prevent a lot of money from becoming a little." The odds against a speculator turning a big profit and losing everything are approximately 25 to 1. No one in the financial world can show you how to turn a little money into a lot in a short period of time—it just does not happen.

7. *Reliably Unpredictable*. Few experts have ever known what is going to happen to a class of securities two years from now, let alone 15 years from now.

8. *Hope Is Not Reality*. "The immature mind has a regrettable tendency to believe, as actually true, that which it hopes to be true."

9. *There Is No Warning*. No one rings a bell to warn you that prices have hit a high and that they will now come down hard and fast from here.

10. *History (Kinda) Repeats*. "History does in a vague way repeat itself, but it does so slowly and ponderously, and with an infinite number of surprising variations."

11. *The Primary Purpose of a Business* . . . "is to make money . . . Almost anyone knows this with the top part of his brain. But there are only a few valuable young men who also know this all up and down their spinal column. Most businessmen imagine that they are in business to make money, and that this is their chief reason for being in business, but more often than not, they are gently kidding themselves. Some of them are to make a fine product, give employment, make oneself famous . . ."

12. *The Second Generation*. "Great family fortunes seldom last long." Occasionally, the heirs spend all of the money, but they usually lose it in bad investments. Too often, the second generation gets it in its head to try to double the value of the estate. The aim of a trust is to preserve capital and produce income. It is not to make a killing.

13. *The Agony of Defeat.* There is no body of literature out there that can make you feel the personal pain of losing your own money. You have to know that kind of hurt in order to avoid it again in the future.

14. *On Not Conceding Defeat.* "It is easy to take a small profit, but taking a small loss is frequently just a good intention." You either wind up riding the loss down to the bottom, or you throw good money after bad and make the situation even worse.

15. *Another Investor Pathology.* A certain type of investor sells stocks at a profit only to reinvest in other stocks. They are economical souls who do not believe in frittering away their money, but they keep everything on the line all of the time. So, when the market goes bust, so do they.

16. *The Average Investor* . . . loses money. Period. It is statistical fact.

17. *Boredom* . . . is a good attribute for a long-term investor.

18. *Watch Out for Revenue Bonds.* Revenue bonds that are not backed by insurance can be a hazard over long periods of time. Railroad and canal bonds were once solid and conservative fixed income investments, and then one day they stopped paying because people found other ways of transporting themselves and their goods.

19. *On Dollars and Sense.* Take care of the pennies and the dollars will take care of themselves is more than a half-truth . . . and at least as accurate is to take care of the millions and the pennies will take care of themselves.

Interview Notes
with PIMCO CEO Mohammad El-Arian

<u>Key Insights</u>:

1. *Investing in the Future.* Mohammad El-Arian advises two key elements of any investment: (1) know your investment objective (and it is not "to make money"), such as to provide for retirement funds, build a house, or pay for college; and (2) be very clear about what mistake you can afford to make.
2. *Types of Investments.* El-Arian believes inflation hedges and significant overseas investments are keys to a diverse portfolio. Half of all S&P500 companies' revenues come from overseas.

Fool's Gold: How the Bold Dream of a Small Tribe at J.P Morgan Was Corrupted by Wall Street Greed and Unleashed a Catastrophe
by Gillian Tett
(New York: Free Press, 2009)

<u>Key Insights</u>:

1. *Where Chance, Opportunity, and Ambition Meet.* "Sometimes in life you just get a huge break, and you just have to grab it and run with it."
2. *The Downside of Financial Innovation.* There is no patent protection for financial innovations, so when a financial institution innovates, it must act quickly to realize its gains before the inevitable competition copies its innovation and catches up.

3. *Why Banks Are Regulated.* The product of a bank is money, and money is not just a product in the traditional sense; it also serves a public utility function.

4. *The Limits of Forecasting Models.* Models are useful, but people must also use their judgment, intuition, and common sense to address issues that models cannot.

5. *All Risk Cannot Be Eliminated.* There is no point in running a bank on the assumption that the financial equivalent of a meteor will hit your industry, company, or the overall economy. Catastrophes will occur, and some will be unknown prior to their occurring. You need to run your business, mitigate against known risks, and diversify your holdings as best you can.

Grande Expectations: A Year in the Life of Starbucks' Stock by Karen Blumenthal (New York: Three Rivers Press, 2007)

Key Insights:

1. *The Amateur Investor's Fallacy.* "Many of us venture into the Oz-like place called Wall Street on our own, in our spare time, hoping we can somehow defy the odds and generate better returns than the broader market itself. We do this knowing full well we would never challenge Tiger Woods to a golf game ... with a realistic expectation of winning, but somehow it seems okay to try to match wits with Wall Street professionals and all their technology, agility, and experience."

2. *Equities Versus Stock Prices.* "There's a big difference between a good company and a good stock."

3. *"Windowdressing"*—a term used to describe why mutual fund managers pick up a hot name stock at the end of

the year to show shareholders in their year-end report that they own that stock. They then quickly dump the stock at the beginning of the next year.

4. *Investing in Entrepreneurs.* Angel investors look for entrepreneurs who are honest people with enough energy and ambition to continue to build their companies. Entrepreneurs also need to show that their egos will allow them to hire the right people to round out and grow their companies.

5. *A Growth Company's Turning Point.* "For retailers, the turning point in the stock market usually came sometime after they opened about half the stores they could possibly open . . . Once investors came to believe the company had matured and growth was permanently braking, the market could be ruthless. Not only would the stock price tumble, but the P/E ratio would sink from its lofty perch, even if the company continued to increase earnings at an above-average rate. The combined effect of a compressing P/E ratio and a slowing growth rate was a stock that could skitter sideways or slide, sometimes for years on end." To avoid that slippery slope, a growth company must convince investors that the company's future potential is far from realized.

6. *Momentum Investors* . . . "knew that stocks in the rise tended to keep climbing—at least until something happened and they started to fall." And when they fall, they fall hard and fast.

7. *Stock Picking Criteria.* Most fund managers have a basic fund picking formula, and when a stock ceases to fit the criteria, they sell it. A highly successful fund group called TWC looked for:

a.   Companies with products that dominated their industries (or with a cost advantage that undercut the competition);

b.   Companies with a business that was hard to copy; and

c.   Management groups that had a winning record.

8.   *On Earnings.* Meeting quarterly earnings forecasts is more important to a stock's short-term performance than return on equity, dividend yield, or any other measurement. Having a great quarter but missing earnings by a penny can slam a stock's price in the short run.

Naked Economics: Undressing the Dismal Science by Charles Wheelan (New York: W. W. Norton and Company, 2010)

Key Insights:

1.   *Government's Economic Goals*:
     a.   Economic growth,
     b.   High employment, and
     c.   Avoid inflation.

2.   *On Unchecked Capitalism.* Even Milton Friedman said that unfettered markets lead to deeply flawed outcomes. Markets do a lousy job of managing communal resources. Government has to police the commons, with the commons being all of the areas that individuals and businesses ignore, thinking that others will do them.

3.   *What Government Does Well.* Government does well in areas that no one else can, such as basic research, courts, policing, parks management, and the military. A basic rule of thumb is that if private industry can do

something, it should do it—not government. The main difference between the private sector and government is, "The private sector allocates resources where they will earn the highest return . . . (and) government allocates resources wherever the political process takes them."

4. *The Key to Capitalism* . . . is that it aligns individual self-interest in a way that leads to a thriving and ever improving standard of living for most (though not all) of society. Markets are aligned with our self-interested nature, and they are successful at motivating us to reach our potential within them. "We work harder when we benefit directly from our work, and that hard work often yields significant societal gains."

5. *Sharing the Economic Pie.* A growing economic pie is most important for those with the smallest slices of the pie. Busboys, not brain surgeons, get laid off in recessions. Policies that guarantee some pie for everyone slow the growth of the pie itself. The United States, for example, has a higher per capita income than France, but there are more U.S. children living in poverty than in France.

6. *Economics Rule Number 1.* Economics assumes that individuals weigh the costs and benefits of all that we do, and we take actions to make ourselves as well off as possible.

7. *On Economic Preferences.* As people get wealthier, preferences for luxury goods and non-essential things (such as sports, entertainment, and fine wines) increase. It is bad economics to impose our preferences on individuals whose lives are much different than ours.

8. *Small Differences in Skill = Big Differences in Compensation.* In large markets small differences in talent can lead to

huge disparities in compensation. Think Michael Jordan or Google.

9. *What the Market Delivers.* "The market is like evolution; it is an extraordinarily powerful force that delivers its strength from rewarding the swift, strong, and smart." That said, two of the most perfectly adapted species on the planet are the mouse and the roach. Similarly, Playboy, Hooters, McDonalds, and Tobacco companies are results of a market delivering what we want, not what we need in any moral sense.

10. *On Mergers.* Two-thirds of all mergers do not add value to the merged firms, and one-third of mergers actually decrease the value of the merged firms.

11. *Cold Blooded Capitalism.* "If you build a better mousetrap, the world will beat a path to your door; if you make the old mousetrap, it's time to start firing people."

12. *The Best Tax Systems* . . . are:
    a. Broad (i.e., not targeted at a narrow segment of the population),
    b. Simple, and
    c. Fair (i.e., affects similar people the same).

13. *Why No One Likes Government.* No one ever likes the umpire, but you need one in order to play the game. People do not like the United States government here in the United States, but our administration, courts, and legal systems are the envy of the rest of the world. You have to bribe someone to get something done in a lot of countries. In a well run society like the United States, public institutions facilitate production, whereas in poorly run societies, public institutions confiscate and actually stifle production.

14. *Human Capital* . . . accounts for 75% of our economy and creates a virtuous cycle. Smart people produce

smart children . . . Human capital leads to gains in productivity—we produce more in less time at a higher quality than we did in the past. High human capital societies have fewer children but invest more in each child.

15. *On Poverty.* Although 20% of children are poor, and 40% of black children are poor, today's poor live at a level equivalent to the level of the top 10 percent of society a century ago. A rising standard of living is relatively new, because in the Dark Ages from 500—1,000 A.D., there was zero productivity growth.

16. *Investing Surprises.* In investing, "it's the things you can't predict that matter," which is why diversification and a long-term time horizon are the best ways to maximize your chances for a good return on your investment.

17. *On Recessions.* In the long term, recessions can be good because they purge less productive ventures out of the system.

18. *International Trade.* Trade is good at the macro level for all parties involved. For someone working in a sweatshop, it is not desirable employment, but it beats the alternatives of prostitution or subsistence farming, and it provides an opportunity for the next generation to climb the next rung on the economic ladder.

19. *Time Versus Money.* As you get wealthier, time becomes more valuable than money, and you will pay someone to free up your time for you to do what you want with it.

CHAPTER 4:
POPULAR FICTION

"Sometimes stories cry out to be told in such loud voices
that you write them just to shut them up."

—Stephen King

Watchlist
by Jeffery Deaver, et. al
(New York: Vanguard Press, 2009)

Key Insights:

1. *On Checking Emotions*. In a competitive contest, you give up your advantage if you allow emotion to trump self-control.
2. *Be Like Beethoven*. "Hear the full, true symphony."
3. *Achievement Requires Persistence*. "There is no giant step that does it. It takes a lot of little steps."
4. *Turning Fantasy into Reality*. "Fantasies exist so that we might strive to make them reality."
5. *The Discipline of Planning*. "He had been mulling over the solution, but had yet to come to a final decision. Time had passed without him acting, but he trusted that his path would become clear, in due course. (He) was a

deliberate man, and that was one of the reasons he was so successful. Put simply, he planned, where others did not. His modus operandi was goal-oriented behavior, whether his goal was losing weight or building weapons of mass destruction."

6. *The Freedom to Choose*. Jean Paul Sartre said, "One always has a choice, if only in how to die."

7. *On Self-Control*. "The wise control themselves, and thus they control the world."—The Buddha.

The Shakeout
by Ken Follett
(New York: The Armchair Detective Library, 1990)

<u>Key Insight</u>:

1. *Your Environment Can Define You*. "Your personality has been molded . . . by your work environment, where energy and poise count, and compassion is a low-profit enterprise."

Dark of the Moon
by John Sanford
(New York: G. P. Putnam's Sons, 2007)

<u>Key Insights</u>:

1. *Rules of Life's Playing Field*. "God made the rules and then even he doesn't break them."

2. *Dynamics of Small Groups*. "In small towns or groups, everyone has a little trouble with everyone else sooner or later but you get over it and you're friends again."

3. *There Are No Slam Dunks in Life.* Sure things always seem to have a way of introducing a previously unknown element of failure in them that must always be factored into one's decisions.

Rules of Vengeance
by Christopher Reich
(New York: Random House, 2009)

Key Insight:

1. *Nice Guys Finish* … "Mikhail Borzoi was not a nice man. Nice men did not control the world's largest producer of aluminum. Nice men did not amass a fortune worth some $20 billion, and that was after the stock market crash. Nice men did not rise from an impoverished childhood to stand at the president's side and be among the three candidates certain to take his place in the next election. Not in Russia. In Russia, nice men got trampled, chewed up, and spit out."

Run for Your Life
by James Patterson and Michael Ledwidge
(New York: Little, Brown, and Company, 2009)

Key Insights:

1. *Shouldering the Burden.* "The cup was heavy, yes—it would crush most men. Only an equally strong resolve, like his own, could bear it."
2. *Keep Your Enemies Close to You.* "The enemies we cannot kill, we must caress, and deception is the art of war."

3. *One Perspective on Life.* "I thought of all the pictures I had . . . All the happy moments, frozen and captured forever. That was it, wasn't it? What life was all about. What could never be taken away. The moments shared with family and the people you loved."

Phantom Prey
by John Sanford
(New York: G. P. Putnam's Sons, 2008)

Key Insights:

1. *Accumulating Intelligence.* Investigations reach a tipping point where everything makes sense if they are approached in a certain way. Every source has a little bit to add to the story, the conclusion is not reached until enough sources have contributed, and then the answer becomes obvious.

2. *Measuring Risk and Reward.* The potential profit from a certain activity has to be weighed against the odds of receiving a reward for that activity, the size of that reward, and the amount of principle you have put at risk to gain that reward.

3. *The Entrepreneur's Mindset.* "Most successful business people are sociopathic—they don't let a lot get in their way. Anyone who's built a business has hurt people."

4. *Life's Winners and Losers* . . . are sometimes separated by a very thin line.

Never Look Away
by Linwood Barclay
(New York: Dell, 2011)

Key Insights:

1. *Controlling Your Enemies.* "It's the old axiom about having your enemies in the tent with you pissing out, instead of their being outside pissing in."
2. *Less Is More.* "In many ways, even minus a hand, he was better at this than he'd ever been before. Less cocky, more cautious."

Too Close To Home
by Linwood Barclay
(New York: Bantam Books, 2009)

Key Insight:

1. *Be Wary of Attention.* "It (is) very rare someone's life (gets) better after being quoted in the newspaper."

Lone Wolf
by Linwood Barclay
(New York: Bantam Books, 2006)

Key Insight:

1. *Human Resources.* "One of the things I've learned, when I was in a law firm, and being mayor of a town . . . your personnel problems are always your biggest headaches."

Rules of Deception
by Christopher Reich
(New York: First Anchor Books, 2008)

<u>Key Insights</u>:

1. *Risky Business.* An addiction to risk can only lead to ruin—it takes only one slip to lose it all.

2. *Do Not Eavesdrop.* "Those who listen at closed doors rarely hear good of themselves."

3. *What Really Matters.* "He refused to be defined by his possessions . . . It was actions that mattered."

4. *Our Societal Contract.* "We all (have) a contract with society to treat our fellow man fairly and to obey the laws. Break that contract, go outside the boundaries of fair play, then all bets were off."

5. *What Is Yours Alone.* "Every subject's duty is the king's; but every subject's soul is his own."

6. *On Pushing Back.* Hitler gave two sets of order in the initial assault on the Rhineland. If the French would have resisted, he would have retreated, and Germany would have suffered a devastating defeat. But, the French did not push back.

7. *Many Baby Steps.* You do not have to be great to achieve. You just have to keep going towards your goal.

Fear No Evil
by Allison Brennan
(New York: Ballantine Books, 2007)

Key Insights:

1. *A Good Life Philosophy.* "Love your neighbor as yourself."
2. *On Responsibility.* "Sometimes he wished he could explode . . . But he couldn't. People depended on his stability, particularly his family."

Wicked Prey
by John Sanford
(New York: G. P. Putnam's Sons, 2009)

Key Insights:

1. *Taking Advantage.* "He adopted any advantage, or possible advantage. That's why he'd survived."
2. *Risk/Reward.* The payoff must *always* be worth the risk. "They always hit at the moment when they'd get the most money and there was the least chance of getting caught."
3. *On Sound Operations.* "They have a reputation for being bold on strategy and careful on tactics." "(They) always work off of a plan, bold, but very careful."
4. *On Getting Things Done.* "As a young girl, she'd learned that if she decided to do something, it was best to do it immediately; otherwise, somebody would stop you from doing it, or you'd start thinking too much and chicken out."

The Program
by Stephen White
(New York: Dell, 2001)

Key Insights:

1. *Facing Your Fears.* "His fear never overrides his will."
2. *Life's Ups and Downs.* "Life is what it is ... mostly (we're) blessed. Come tomorrow or the next day, this passes and the good life goes on.

Beautiful Lies
by Lisa Unger
(New York: Vintage Books, 2008)

Key Insights:

1. *You Can Never Go Back.* "Once the mind glimpses enlightenment, it can never go back."
2. *Who Do You Love and Who Loves You?* How many people truly care about you—feel good when you feel good, bad when you hurt? "People who would walk away from their lives for a little while to help you with yours. Not many."
3. *Your Actions Reflect on More People Than Just You.* "When someone is invested in your well-being, like your parents, for example, you become responsible for them in a way. Anything you do to hurt yourself hurts them ... You're not really free when people care about you; not if you care about them."
4. *On Mentally Shutting Down.* "The mind can't handle emotions like grief and terror for any sustained period of time, so it takes some downtime."

5. *On Adaptability*. "It is not the strongest among us who survive. Nor is it the most intelligent. It is those among us who are most adaptable to change."

4th of July
by James Patterson and Maxine Paetro
(New York: Little, Brown, and Company, 2005)

Key Insight:

1. *The Ones We Never Catch*. The really smart maniacs never get caught.

The Burning Wire by Jeffery Deaver
(New York: Simon and Schuster, 2010)

Key Insights:

1. *Avoid Emotional Decision Making*. "Emotion breeds mistake and carelessness."
2. *On Disabilities*. "One of the difficulties with a severe disability that few people focus on is the absence of anything new. The same settings, the same people, the same activities . . . and the same platitudes, the same reassurances . . ."
3. *Remaining in Motion*. "When you move, they can't getcha."
4. *Cool Under Fire*. The good leader remains calm and in control. The weak and insecure are the ones who bluster.
5. *The Hare Krishna Path to Righteousness*: (1) mercy, (2) self-control, (3) honesty, and (4) cleanliness of body and spirit.

6. *Genius = Work More Than Talent.* Thomas Edison said a genius is nothing more than a talented person who does his homework.

7. *Fill Your Brain.* "The more you put in your brain, the more likely you (are) to make connections."

The First Commandment
by Brad Thor
(London: Pocket Books, 2007)

Key Insights:

1. *Wishful Thinking.* "Do not wish ill for your enemy, plan it."
2. *Knowledge Does Not Equal Power.* The application of knowledge equals power.
3. *Seizing Opportunity.* When the window of opportunity opens, you have to seize it.
4. *On Losing Control.* "When a man loses his self-control he is much more susceptible to the control of another."
5. *What Is Happiness?* "Being happy boils down to three things. Something to do. Someone to love. And something to look forward to."
6. *Getting an Edge.* "Even the small advantage is better than no advantage at all."

The Sanctuary
by Raymond Khoury
(New York: Signet, 2008)

Key Insights:

1. *Poise.* "The two men facing him were impatient, and in his experience, poise was as effective a weapon as a sword."

2. *Be Prepared.* "Life turn(s) on a dime. He'd been around long enough to know how true that was."

3. *On the Human Life Span.* Reductions in infant mortality rates have enabled the average human life expectancy to rise from 40 years in the 19th Century, to 50 years at the start of the 20th Century, to 80 years in 21st Century developed countries. "Demographers predicting an upper limit to our expected life spans (have) consistently proven wrong." Natural selection only cared about ensuring humans lived long enough to bear and rear children in a hostile environment to pass their genes to the next generation. Natural selection did not genetically program us to die; we are killed in old age by wear and tear; therefore, science may one day be able to fix our worn out parts and allow us to live much longer life spans.

4. *On Human Population Growth.* It took 80 million years to produce 1 billion humans in the early 1800's, 100 years to reach 2 billion humans in 1930, and every 15 years since 1930 another billion humans have been added. Most of the recent increases have occurred in developing nations, since many developed nations barely produce enough offspring to maintain their populations.

Betrayal
by John Lescroat
(New York: Dutton, 2008)

Key Insight:

1. *Plans Do Not Survive Contact with the Enemy.* "Well, Lieutenant, welcome to the war. Plans are what you

work with before you get there. They give you the illusion you've got some control, and you don't."

24 Declassified: Operation Hell Gate
by Marc Cerasini
(New York: Harper Entertainment, 2005)

Key Insights:

1. *Sound Tactics.* "Instead of waiting for the inevitable attack, an aggressive commander would dispatch pickets to prick his foe into premature action."
2. *What Favor?* "If a man demands something in return for his help, that's not generosity, is it? That's a transaction."
3. *The Nomadic Code.* "Nomadic Pashtuns were raised according to an ancient tribal code . . . which stressed honor, courage, bold action, and self-reliance."
4. *In Politics* . . . impressions are always more important than results.
5. *Middle Management Hell.* If you make the right choice, you get a pat on the back or even a citation—mainly, you get to keep your job. If you make the wrong choice, your career is over.

Degree of Guilt
by Richard North Patterson
(New York: St. Martin's Press, 1992)

Key Insights:

1. *On Expectations.* "Always expect people to be what they've been in the past . . . Being surprised is a sin, professionally."

2. *The Child Within*. Sometimes it helps to view adults as a five-year old. Many adult motivations can be traced to childhood.

3. *An Emotion Alternative*. "Sarcasm is the safe alternative to anger."

4. *Margaret Thatcher's Leadership Style*. "People reacted to her, not the other way around."

5. *The Human Web*. There's an enormous human current you can plug into.

6. *The Fraud Within*. "Inside every self-assured professional lives a frightened neurotic who prays that he can succeed before (people) discover the fraud."

7. *Money* . . . makes you free.

The Last Patriot
by Brad Thor
(New York: Pocket Books, 2008)

Key Insights:

1. *Forever Young*. "Up until the 1950's, American children yearned for adulthood. When their time came to be adults, they stepped into their role proudly, leaving childhood behind and taking up the mantles of responsibility, honor, and dignity. They embraced and championed the ideals of those who came before them while valiantly tackling new ideas and problems that their families, communities, and nations faced. Those days were long gone. Americans now shunned adulthood, preferring to stay in a state of perpetual adolescence. By failing to move forward with grace and dignity, they left a gaping hole in American society. They treated relationships like disposable lighters, tossing marriages away when

they ran out of gas. Children were left without families, and even worse, they were left without adults who could be role models of responsible behavior. With this lack of willingness to step forward and embrace adulthood, the nation had lost sight of its core values and ideals. In its place had morphed an every man and woman for himself in which materialism was placed before spirituality and submission to God."

2. *On the Ground Awareness.* Operations that have too many degrees of separation from the planners will fail miserably.

3. *Watch Your Tongue.* "While the words are left unspoken, you are the master of them; when once they are spoken, they are the master of you."

4. *On Silence.* Most people are uncomfortable with silence and will fill the void if you keep your own mouth shut.

5. *On Value.* Products have two of the following three attributes—fast, good, or cheap—but you cannot typically get all three attributes in one product.

6. *Action Creates Intelligence.* Flush an issue out into the open to gain information from it.

7. *On Complaints.* "The dogs may bark but the caravan moves on."

8. *You Can't Always Get What You Want.* "When what we want doesn't happen, we must learn to want what does."

Final Venture
by Michael Ridpath
(New York: Penguin Books, 2001)

Key Insights:

1. *In Early Stage Companies, People Are the Key.* "Venture capitalists are proud of backing people, not businesses.

Once you begin to doubt the person, then it is very hard not to doubt the business."

2. *Don't Throw Good Money After Bad.* "We took a risk with the first two million. That's what we're supposed to do as venture capitalists. But the market's moving away from us, and the entrepreneur's losing perspective. The deal looks different. It would be a mistake to drop another three million now."

3. *Take Your Losses.* "When a deal turns sour, you should take your losses. We've learned that lesson over the years the hard way."

4. *Character Counts.* "In life there were some people you could trust and some you couldn't, and I thought it was important to be one of those you could."

5. *Have An Escape Hatch.* Don't make promises that box you in. "As a venture capitalist, you always have to leave a way out. Circumstances change, the unforeseen always happens."

6. *Know How and When to Say "No."* "Years in venture capital had taught him to say 'no' firmly and finally . . ." On the other hand, "venture capitalists spend so much time saying 'no,' it is always satisfying when there is a chance to say, 'yes.'"

7. *Venture Capital's Age-Old Mystery.* "Which comes first, the prototype or the money?"

8. *No Deal Is Ever Perfect.*

9. *Money Talks.* "In America, you've got to have money. If you have money, people take notice. And it's got to be big money."

The Secret Supper
by Javier Sierra
(New York: Atria Books, 2004)

<u>Key Insights</u>:

1. *Da Vinci's Habits and Disciplines.* Leonardo Da Vinci spent his days carrying a notebook around with his ideas, making observations of everything that came to mind. "For Leonardo, everything merited attention, everything held within itself traces of the science of life." He dreamed of devices to help with everyday life. To the frustration of his assistants, he had a jeweler's eye and studied everything in minute detail. Da Vinci sought perfection, and revised his work countless times.

2. *Enemies Matter.* "Without Judas's treason, Christ would've never achieved his destiny."

3. *Why Da Vinci Stayed Single.* "If you go with a woman, you'll divide your gifts in two, and in three if you have a child, and if you bring two or three children into this world, you'll lose your gifts entirely."

4. *On Faith.* "Their strength lies in that they are abstract sacraments. Whoever perceives them from within feels a blow to the chest and an all-invading joy. You know you're saved when you feel that force inside you."

5. *Art for the Illiterate.* Da Vinci created canvases to bring sacred stories to life for the many people of his time who could not read.

1st *to Die*
by James Patterson
(New York: Warner Books, 2001)

Key Insights:

1. *Childhood's End.* "There comes a point in everybody's life when you realize the stakes have suddenly changed. The carefree ride of your life slams into a stone wall; all those years of merely bouncing along, life taking you where you want to go, abruptly end."

2. *On Having Fun.* "When I'm drawing my last breath, I won't be thinking about all those fancy degrees or conferences I spoke at. You only have a few times in your life to really cut loose, so you might as well take them when they come."

The Associate
by John Grisham
(New York: Dell, 2009)

Key Insights:

1. *Kissing Up.* "The first gunner appeared. There is at least one in every class, whether it's first-year contracts in law school or a group of fresh recruits on Wall Street. A gunner sits in the front row, asks complicated questions, sucks up to whoever happens to be at the podium, works every angle, cuts throats for better grades, stabs backs to make law review, interviews only at the top-rated firms regardless of how bad their reputations might be, and arrives at the firm with every intention of making

partner before anyone else in his class. Gunners succeed magnificently; most make partner."

2. *Knowledge Is Power*. "Information is crucial. The more they watch and listen, the more they know about me. If they know what I eat, drink, wear, listen to, and who I talk to and hang out with and where I like to shop and browse and sneak away to, then they might one day be able to use it all to their advantage."

Roadside Crosses
by Jeffery Deaver
(New York: Simon and Schuster, 2010)

Key Insights:

1. *Strength Through Adversity*. A former gang member who became a cop was the most focused and calmest member of the force. Going through a hard experience toughens you for the rest of life that follows and makes future difficult experiences easier to manage.

2. *Extrovert Versus Introvert*. "The distinction between extrovert and introvert is about attitude. Does the subject act first and then assess the results (an extrovert), or reflect before acting (introvert)? Information gathering is carried out either by trusting the five senses and verifying data (sensing) or relying on hunches (intuition). Decision making occurs either by objective, logical analysis (thinking) or by making choices based on empathy (feeling)."

3. *On Liars*. There are several types of liars. "Manipulators or 'high Machiavellians,' see absolutely nothing wrong with lying; they use deceit as a tool to achieve their goals in love, business, politics or crime and are very, very good

at deception. Other types include social liars, who lie to entertain; adaptors, insecure people who lie to make positive impressions; and actors, who lie for control."

4. *The Seeds of Violence.* "The tendency to violence in young people almost always comes from rage, not watching movies or television." Media exposure may only numb a child to violence's consequences if they see too much of it at an early age.

5. *What Is Real?* The average hard core gamer spends 30 hours a week online, and many spend double that amount of time. Twenty percent of gamers think the physical world is just a place to eat and sleep, while the synthetic world is their real world.

6. *On Pain and Fear.* It is better to confront issues of pain and fear with children rather than deny or defer those issues with them.

7. *On Preparing Children.* "You always hope, you pray, that you give your children the resources they need, the attitude, the courage. That's what it's all about, after all. Not fighting their battles, but getting them prepared to fight on their own. Teaching them to make judgments, to think for themselves."

Gone for Good
by Harlan Coben
(New York: Dell, 2003)

Key Insights:

1. *Life on the Streets.* "A kid living on the street is a bit like—and please pardon the analogy here—a weed. The

longer he's on the street, the harder it is to pull him out by the root ... Early screening and preventive treatment is the key to long-term survival."

2. *Surviving Adolescence.* "In hindsight, highschool—adolescence, if you will—feels a little like protracted combat. You just need to survive, get through it, come out of it okay."

Gone Tomorrow
by Lee Child
(New York: Dell, 2010)

Key Insights:

1. *The Wealth Hierarchy.* "He had become a single-figure billionaire. Next step was to become a double-figure billionaire. He didn't make it. It was a tight bottleneck. Everyone wanted to squeeze through, and there wasn't room for everyone to succeed."

2. *Before You Attack.* "When contemplating an offensive, the very first thing you must plan is your inevitable retreat."

3. *Standard Tactical Doctrine.* "Assault from the high ground."

4. *Sneaky Tactical Doctrine.* "(Double) back to positions previously written off as abandoned."

5. *Definition of a Rich Man.* "To have everything you need."

The Devil's Company
by David Liss
(New York: Ballantine Books, 2009)

Key Insights:

1. *Fear of the Unknown.* "Darkness holds far greater terrors than any monstrosity, no matter how terrible, revealed in the light."
2. *On Chance.* "Fortune is a fickle goddess and can strike blows where no one expects and elevate the mendicant to great heights."
3. *How to Start a Fashion Trend.* "Give your goods away to a few fashionable people who have the power to set trends, and the trend is set."
4. *Avoid Surprises.* "Surprise leads to three things . . . inefficiency, . . . disorder, (and) diminished returns."
5. *On Truthfulness.* "Those who speak the truth must face the brickbats of resentment." Actions that preserve your place in society may betray your soul.
6. *Company* . . . derives from the Latin *com panis*—the act of baking bread together—a collective union of effort.
7. *On Anger.* Separate yourself from your own anger when making decisions or it will consume you.

Skin
by Ted Dekker
(Brentwood, Tennessee: Thomas Nelson, 2007)

Key Insight:

1. *On Human Perception and Misperception.* "How did Hitler deceive a nation? How can one group of people

look at the world and see one thing, and another see something completely different? One sees a town, and another a desert. One sees beauty, another sees chaos."

Carte Blanche
by Jeffery Deaver
(New York: Simon and Schuster, 2011)

Key Insights:

1. *The Devil Is in the Details.* "Small clues save you. Small errors kill."
2. *There's Money to Be Made in Strange Places.* "Disposing of what people no longer wanted had always been, and forever would be, a profitable endeavor."
3. *On Adulation.* "If you want adulation, just give away money. The more desperate they are, the more they love you."
4. *Be the Flower, Not the Bee.* "Seduction in tradecraft is like seduction in love; it works best if you make the object of your desire come to you. Nothing ruins your efforts faster than desperate pursuit."
5. *On Wisdom.* "Being older is strength. It's experience, judgment, discernment, knowing your resources. Youth is mistake and impulse."
6. *On Gathering Intelligence.* "Most of your job is going to involve waiting. I hope you're a patient man."

The Final Detail
by Harlan Coben
(New York: Dell Publishing, 1999)

<u>Key Insights</u>:

1. *An Easy Way to Riches*. Redistributing wealth, "the act of moving money around without creation or production or making anything new, (is) incredibly profitable."
2. *On the Food Chain*. "God created a world where the only way to survive is to kill. Period. We all kill. Even the strict vegetarians have to plow fields. You don't think plowing kills small animals and insects?" The universal truth about nature is, "You either kill or you die."

Saint
by Ted Dekker
(Nashville, Tennessee: WestBow Press, 2006)

<u>Key Insights</u>:

1. *Elements of a Successful Attack*. "Assault has three allies: speed, surprise, and power."
2. *Emotions* . . . are ultimately nothing more than chemical reactions in the brain.
3. *A Sense of Wonder*. "Unless you become like a child, you can't do much of anything good in this world."
4. *Be Like Spiderman*. "Accepting your true identity means understanding that you are a stranger to this world." Do not let the world change you; instead, you need to change the world.
5. *On Zen*. Warriors and spiritual masters have proven that a human being can:

a. Focus the mind,
b. Shut out pain, and
c. Control emotions.

Hold Tight
by Harlan Coben
(New York: Penguin Books, 2008)

<u>Key Insights</u>:

1. *The Limitations of Parental Influence.* "In the end, we're just (our children's) caretakers . . . We get them for a little while and then they live their lives. I just want him to stay alive and healthy until we let him go. The rest will be up to him."

2. *On Rough Childhoods.* "That early rage turned to focus . . . You either channeled it out or you internalized it."

3. *On Rough Teenage Years.* "This too shall pass—and it will pass quickly."

4. *Who Owns You?* "They say possessions own you. Not so. Loved ones own you. You are forever held hostage once you care so much."

5. *When You Are Desperate* . . . "you can try to mask it, but the smell permeates."

6. *Coming from Nothing.* "Sometimes it's easier (to come from nothing). Ambition is natural when you don't have anything. You know what you're driving for."

The 37ᵗʰ Hour
by Jodi Compton
(New York: Dell, 2005)

Key Insights:

1. *Focus.* "A major investigation is frenetic and distracting. In the middle of it all, you've got to ignore the fire and the whirlwind and listen for a still, small voice . . . the still small voice comes from the oldest and wisest part of the mind."
2. *It Shows on Your Face.* "The older we get, the more our faces reflect our lives and our thoughts."
3. *Some Things Are Out of Our Control.* "Childhood is like the weather: you can talk about it all you want, but there's nothing you can do about it."

Twelve Red Herrings
by Jeffrey Archer
(New York: HarperCollins, 1994)

Key Insights:

1. *Know Your People.* "Never make the mistake of imagining that your friends and your colleagues (are) necessarily the same animals."
2. *Cash Is King.* "The takeover has been agreed, and at half the price it would have cost me only a year ago . . . Those of us who are still in possession of cash have no fear of the recession."
3. *Hard Work Trumps Talent.* In art, no matter how talented an artist may be, it is industry and dedication that mark the few who succeed from the many who fail.

High Crimes
by Joseph Finder
(New York: Avon Books, 1998)

Key Insights:

1. *"Fruit of the Poisoned Tree."* The *Constitution's* Fourth Amendment "protects us from unreasonable government searches. So any evidence obtained in violation of the Fourth Amendment must be excluded from a criminal trial."

2. *Principle Versus Practice.* "In the classroom, . . . we can talk about principle. In the courtroom, you put aside whatever the hell you believe in and fight with every goddamned scrap of ammunition you've got."

3. *Appreciating What You Have.* "Happy marriages were only really appreciated by those who'd been married, badly, already."

4. *Old Russian Proverb on Failure.* "The first pancake is always a lump."

5. *Men and Friends.* "Friends? Guys in their forties rarely have more than a couple of friends . . . Men aren't like women. They get married and get buried in their jobs and sort of fall off the face of the earth."

The Betrayal Game
by David Robbins
(New York: Bantam Books, 2009)

Key Insights:

1. *On Bending One's Principles.* "The devil . . . must be invited in." "Deals with the devil" end up with him always demanding more.

2. *Why Revolutions Are So Bloody.* "Reformers and revolutionaries transform the entire system of governance. Wealth and authority shift hands dramatically. That makes for very big, very dedicated enemies. People who've got everything to lose."

3. *On Violence.* Karl Marx said, "Without violence, nothing is ever accomplished in history."

4. *Why Fidel Castro Succeeded.* Castro had extraordinary magnetism and persuasiveness. "No other man . . . would have sailed from Mexico with 82 others, not a one of them with military experience, to conquer a nation." Castro took risks that other revolutionaries did not. "Lenin waited out the beginnings of the Russian Revolution in the safety of Zurich. Stalin was a military administrator during the Russian Civil War. Mao controlled armies but never suffered privations. Khrushchev didn't fight in World War II. Hitler yelled in bear halls while others slit throats for him. Castro slept with a rifle barrel tucked under his chin."

5. *The Downside of Accomplishment.* "A man with no enemies hasn't done shit in his life."

6. *On Heroes.* "The vast majority of folks who made history were just ordinary people in extraordinary times."

7. *On Politics.* "Every decision (is) strained through the needs of a nation . . . Compromise is the rule."

8. *The Assassin* . . . sits right on the divide of whether individuals or events are more important in history. The fundamental question is: does an assassin's action change a country's course or not?

The Inner Circle
by Brad Meltzer
(New York: Grand Central Publishing, 2011)

<u>Key Insights</u>:

1. *Who You Really Are.* "In life, there's the way you act when you know people are watching. And, then there's the way you act when no one's watching, which, let's be honest, is the real you."

2. *On Presidential Power.* "Name one person who went up against a sitting President and walked away the same way they walked in."

3. *The Virtue of Patience.* Ben Franklin said, "He that can have patience, can have what he will."

4. *Give Thanks.* Start every day being thankful for something—it will remind you of your place in the world.

5. *When Character Meets Opportunity.* History chooses its moments, events, and people. "The only ones we read about are the ones who face that situation, and fight that situation, and find out who they really are." "History doesn't choose individual people. History chooses everyone. Every day." It is how we respond to history's call that matters.

6. *Live Big.* "Big lives (require) big sacrifice."

Boneman's Daughters
by Ted Dekker
(New York: Center Street, 2009)

Key Insights:

1. *Separating War's Forest from Its Trees.* In the heat of battle it is hard to see the connection between one's actions and the success or failure of a larger strategy. "History will one day get us far enough from this mess to tell us what we did here."
2. *On Fatherhood.* "Millions, hundreds of millions of children grow up without a father nearby. In whole cultures, fathers are less accessible to their children than in ours. During the times of patriarchs, times of war, the birth of our nation . . ."
3. *Troubling Incarceration Trends.* "On January 1, 2008, for the first time in history, a full one percent of all Americans were locked behind bars."

The Bride Collector
by Ted Dekker
(New York: Center Street, 2010)

Key Insights:

1. *Obsessiveness* . . . is the only difference between good and great.
2. *On Mental Health.* Mental illness is much more widespread than commonly thought. Over 700,000 mentally ill citizens are jailed each year.

3. *Good Doctoring* . . . "is a process of eliminating potential diseases until a physician (is) left with the most likely ailment to explain the symptoms."
4. *Under Pressure.* Some thoughts emerge only in response to pressured speech.
5. *On Madness.* "It's human nature to encourage the status quo and shun those who see life differently . . . But madness (can prove) to be an alternative sanity of the highest order, a better way of looking at the world that (goes) against the grain but is, in fact, truth."

Cutting Edge
by Allison Brennan
(New York: Ballantine Books, 2009)

Key Insights:

1. *Watch Your Habits.* "A regular schedule. Criminals love habits. They were easy to monitor, giving stalkers and others valuable information about their prey."
2. *Checking Emotions.* "A lot of cops burn out too fast because they don't learn to tame their emotions." "Hate is a negative emotion. It turns us inside out and we make mistakes."
3. *No Compromise.* "When core values of two people differ, there is no way to see eye to eye."

Eight in the Box
by Raffi Yessayan
(New York: Ballantine Books, 2010)

Key Insights:

1. *In Tense Moments* . . . when people are watching you, perform some simple ritualistic functions to pull your mind together, build confidence, and show them calm and poise.
2. *Leadership Is Not Always Appreciated.* "Ruby Bridges, who had to walk the gauntlet every day, escorted by federal marshals just to go to her desegregated school in New Orleans . . . Do you think that six-year old girl had someone telling her that they appreciated what she was doing for every black child in America?"
3. *Don't Chase Power.* In *The Antichrist*, Friedrich Nietzsche said, "What is good? Whatever augments the feeling of power, the will to power, power itself in man. What is evil? Whatever springs from weakness. What is happiness? The feeling that power increases—that resistance is overcome."

Everything's Eventual
by Stephen King
(New York: Pocket Books, 2002)

Key Insights:

1. *On Writing Things Down.* "What you write down sometimes leaves you forever, like old photographs left in the bright sun, fading to nothing but white."

2. *Spread the Light.* "In God's eyes, none of us are really more than flies on strings and all that matters is how much sunshine you can spread along the way."

Think of a Number
by John Verdon
(New York: Broadway Paperbacks, 2010)

<u>Key Insights</u>:

1. *In Lieu of New Information . . . Change Your Mind.* "The main thing was to be aware of the fallibility of the process and be willing to revise the label as new information became available."
2. *Think Much, Act Little.* "He spent more time in the consideration of action than in action, more time in his head than in the world. This had never been a problem in his profession; in truth, it was the very thing that seemed to make him so good . . ."
3. *The Roles We Play.* "People act out certain roles in their lives . . . the scripts (are) consistent and predictable, although generally unconscious and rarely seen as a matter of choice."
4. *The Cost of Action.* "Every act demands its price. And every price comes due."
5. *On Life's Mysteries.* Not everything in life is a puzzle to be solved. Some things are to be embraced, loved, and left unsolved.
6. *Smile!* "Always smile on the phone when you are speaking, because it makes you sound friendlier."
7. *On Deduction.* Sherlock Holmes said, "When you have eliminated the impossible, whatever remains, however improbable, must be the truth."

8. *Don't Ignore Your Doubts*. If you have misgivings about doing something, don't push them aside. Analyze your doubts and weigh them in your decision to act or not, because those doubts are there for a reason.

Fertile Ground
by Ben Mezrich
(New York: Avon, 2001)

Key Insights:

1. *They Know Us Better Than We Know Ourselves*. A consumer goods company "knew everything there was to know about her . . . Her wants, her needs, most of all her pocketbook. What made it open and close, what motivated her to reach inside and grab for that credit card."
2. *Be Realistic*. "One of the cardinal rules of business is to set realistic goals."

Fear the Worst
by Linwood Barclay
(New York: Dell, 2010)

Key Insights:

1. *Handling Life's Setbacks*. "I know about sadness . . . My life has been one sadness after another. But if you wait for all of them to be over before you allow yourself any pleasure, you'll never have any."
2. *Go with the Gut*. Sometimes your gut instinct is better than your decision after weeks of research.

No Time for Goodbye
by Linwood Barclay
(New York: Bantam Books, 2007)

Key Insights:

1. *On Parental Limitations.* One of the toughest things about being a parent is realizing you can't protect them from everything.
2. *When Will the Luck Run Out?* "Life is always asking yourself, when's it coming? Because if it hasn't come for a long, long time, you know you're f'ing due."

Twilight
by Stephanie Meyer
(New York: Little, Brown, and Company, 2005)

Key Insight:

1. *On Decision Making.* "Making decisions was the painful part for me, the part I agonized over. But once the decision was made, I simply followed through—usually with relief that the choice was made. Sometimes the relief was tainted by despair . . . But it was still better than wrestling with the alternatives."

New Moon
by Stephanie Meyer
(New York: Little, Brown, and Company, 2006)

<u>Key Insight</u>:

1. *On Playing the Hand You Are Dealt.* "Like everything in life, I just had to decide what to do with what I was given."

Dead Even
by Brad Meltzer
(New York: William Morrow, 1998)

<u>Key Insights</u>:

1. *Some Things Must Be Earned and Others Not Lost.* Arthur Schopenhauer said, "Fame is something which must be won; honor is something which must not be lost."
2. *Confidence* . . . can be smelled a mile away. It separates those who can close a deal versus those who cannot.
3. *Impressions Matter.* There is power in making a strong impression; people gravitate to a strong impression.
4. *Don't Let 'Em See You Sweat.* Work as hard as you can but make it look easy on the outside.
5. *Prepare for the Worst* . . . and then you will not be surprised if it happens.

The Girl Who Played with Fire
by Stieg Larsson
(New York: Vintage Books, 2009)

Key Insights:

1. *Conservative Investing.* "A smaller, less risky profit was good business."
2. *On Deduction.* "The simplest explanation (is) often the right one."
3. *The Fine Line Between Success and Failure.* When the margin of error is small, things can swing quickly from victory to failure.
4. *Walk Away.* Always retain the ability to walk away "from a situation that is unmanageable. That was a basic rule for survival. Don't lift a finger for a lost cause."

False Impression
by Jeffrey Archer
(New York: St. Martin's Press, 2006)

Key Insights:

1. *FBI Maxim.* "Never believe in coincidences, but never dismiss them."
2. *Patience.* It is a skill developed only after many hours of practice, just like any other skill.
3. *First Impressions.* A great collector makes up his mind in minutes. A scientific survey has shown that men make up their mind to sleep with a woman in eight seconds.

Eclipse
by Stephanie Meyer
(New York: Little, Brown, and Company, 2007)

<u>Key Insights</u>:

1. *On Children.* "You have to let them go their own way eventually . . . You have to let them have their own life."
2. *On Simplicity.* "Something about her simple view of the world cut through all the distractions and pierced right to the truth of things."
3. *Skill or Luck*? "He saw his prosperity as a reward for talent and hard work, rather than acknowledging the luck involved."
4. *The Wise Leader.* "He was known for his wisdom, and for being a man of peace. The people lived well and content in his care."
5. *Right and Wrong.* "The right thing isn't always real obvious. Sometimes the right thing for one person is the wrong thing for someone else."

The Confession
by John Grisham
(New York: Dell, 2010)

<u>Key Insights</u>:

1. *Waiving Your Right to Counsel.* "Innocent people are much likelier to waive their rights during an interrogation. They know they are innocent, and they want to cooperate with the police to prove their innocence. Guilty suspects are more inclined not to cooperate. Seasoned criminals laugh at the police and clam up."

2. *Good Lawyers* . . . work from a long checklist on a legal pad, and they work that list to the bone.
3. *On Turning the Other Cheek.* "It's man's nature to strike back, but the second blow leads to the third, and the fourth."
4. *Economy of Words.* Sometimes, the least number of words you use to achieve your objective, the better off you will be.

Shadow of Death
by William Tapply
(New York: St. Martin's Press, 2001)

Key Insights:

1. *Lacking Trust.* "Mistrust was probably a useful trait for a lawyer, but it was a piss-poor trait for a human being."
2. *Knowing Your Capabilities.* "I know what I can do, and more important, I know what I can't do, and most important of all, I never hesitate to admit it."
3. *Know Your Chance of Success.* "When you're right, go for the kill. When you're wrong, go for the compromise."
4. *It's Better to be Lucky Than Good.* "He'd cashed out of a dot-com start-up . . . less than six months before it crashed and burned." He was just lucky. "It wasn't as if he saw it coming . . ."
5. *Compartmentalize.* "Concentrate on the job at hand no matter what's going on."
6. *Read Every Word.* Everything in a legal document is significant. Everything.

The First Rule
by Robert Crais
(New York: G. P. Putnam's Sons, 2010)

Key Insights:

1. *Staying Ahead of the Game.* "It's not enough to follow the play; "you (have) to be ahead of the action to survive."
2. *On Responsibility.* "You become responsible, forever, for what you have tamed."
3. *Be Forward-Looking.* "Leave the past. Always move forward."
4. *Agility.* "In armed confrontations, speed (is) the difference between life and death."
5. *On Decision Making.* "Access the situation, plan a single action, then commit yourself to that action. A war is won one maneuver at a time."
6. *Make Others Adapt to You.* "One of the first rules of combat (is) that all battle plans change, and the winner (is) usually the guy who forced the changes."

Edge
by Jeffery Deaver
(New York: Simon and Schuster, 2010)

Key Insights:

1. *Be Humble and Magnanimous in Victory.* "Being a good winner gives you a slight advantage psychologically when you play against the same opponent in the future."
2. *Strategic Foresight.* "If you do research up front, you'll be less likely to need tactical firepower later."

3. *Pay Attention.* "Most people are simply extremely unobservant."

4. *A Soothing Personality.* "I tend to be overly polite—stiff, many people say. But a calm, structured attitude gets people's cooperation better than bluster . . ."

5. *Get a Foot in the Door.* "Arguments in doorways are hard to win; your opponent can just step back and close the door." The key is to get the other person to come out with you, or you go in with them, in order to create a sense of commitment.

6. *What's the Goal?* The biggest key to business is knowing, "What's my goal and what's the most efficient way to achieve it? Nothing else matters."

7. *The Key to School.* A motivational hook is necessary to get a student to engage. For example, "when I began to look at classes as a series of incrementally complex games, I devoted myself to the courses intensively."

8. *Be a Little Nervous.* It is okay to be a little afraid in business; the trepidation keeps you aware, alive, and effective.

9. *On Explanations.* "People who explain are weak."

10. *What the Future Holds.* Most things in life follow the path of least resistance. To see the future, just find the least resistant path.

11. *On Observation.* The smart ones watch, listen, and observe.

12. *The Board Game Risk's Instructions.* "Remember that this is a game of defense as well as offense and be prepared to protect the areas which you occupy."

13. *On Good Deeds.* "No good deed goes unpunished."

14. *On Predictions.* "The world is made up of constantly changing knowledge, and in determining the probability

of an event . . . you have to continually readjust your predictions as you learn new bits of information."

15. *On Facing the Enemy.* Emotion is deadly in a competitive contest. "Do whatever you can to get an edge over your opponent."

Hell's Gate
by Richard Crabbe
(New York: Thomas Dunne Books, 2008)

Key Insights:

1. *On Poise.* "It's the one who's calm under pressure who'll be the last one standing . . . Ninety-nine percent of the time it'll be the other guy spraying bullets all over."

2. *Avoid the Gambler's Rush.* "Funny what some men'll do, the risks they'll take for the thrill o' winning. Doesn't mean he's stupid, just that he loves the thrill, convinced he can beat the odds."

3. *It Pays to Be Seen.* "Out an' about. A politician's no good to anybody if you can't see him."

4. *The Perfect Angle.* "(He) thought of those things constantly . . . rolling them around in his head, looking for the perfect angle, that delicate point at which the least leverage might be applied to the greatest advantage."

5. *Keep a Nice Home.* "It can be an ugly world outside . . . I bring a little beauty into my place."

6. *The Role of the Sidekick.* "He trusted (him) about as much as he trusted any man alive. He was a reliable, if somewhat unimaginative, lieutenant, not a bad combination . . ."

7. *Accept Your Losses.* "It was healthier . . . to acknowledge the mistakes, accept the losses, come to terms with failures."

Nothing to Lose
by Lee Child
(New York, Dell 2010)

<u>Key Insights</u>:

1. *What Defines Your Life?* "Everyone's life needed an organizing principle, and relentless forward motion was (his)." "He liked to press on, dead ahead . . ."
2. *Which Way Do You Turn?* "Psychologists figured that the memory center was located in the left brain, and the imagination engine in the right brain. Therefore people unconsciously glanced to the left when they were remembering things, and to the right when they were making stuff up. When they were lying."
3. *Clichés.* "Clichés (are) clichés because they (are) so often true."
4. *On Difficult Conversations.* "The hardest part of any adversarial conversation (is) the beginning. An early answer (is) a good sign. Answering (becomes) a habit."
5. *What Soldiers Fear.* "They fear grotesque wounds. That's all. Amputations, mutilations, burns."
6. *A Recycled World.* "Steel is a wonderful thing . . . It goes around and around. Peugeots and Toyotas from the Gulf might once have been Fords and Chevrolets from Detroit, and they in turn might once have been Rolls-Royces from England or Holdens from Australia.

Or bicycles or refrigerators. Some steel is new, of course, but surprisingly little of it. Recycling is where the action is."

The Spire
by Richard North Patterson
(New York: Henry Holt and Company, 2009)

Key Insights:

1. *Gimme Shelter*. "There's nowhere for a college president to hide."
2. *A Fine Line*. "Sometimes genius and madness feed upon each other."
3. *On Discipline*. The Vietnam War taught some officers "what men are capable of doing when there's no constraint on their impulses or desire."
4. *Questionable Objectivity*. "A man's supposedly objective beliefs are so often a product of his needs."
5. *"Keep Moving Forward"* is the key to advancing in life.
6. *Inclusion*. "The quality of one's decisions isn't enough . . . (people) need to feel they're included."
7. *On Near Misses*. "Sometimes, people forget that all of us live a few feet, or a few seconds, from tragedy—some random accident that just misses us without our even knowing."
8. *Individuality*. "In a very real sense, we all go through life alone."
9. *We Are Not Our Worst Mistakes*. "Men (are) too complex to be defined by the worst moment in their lives."
10. *Self-Knowledge Is Biased*. "Self-knowledge is, at best, imperfect. Never more so than when the entire truth about oneself may be less attractive than one hopes."

11. *On Making Your Own Decisions.* "Sometimes, it's easier when decisions get made for you. It's far more difficult when *you* have to make them, not knowing what else may be out there."

12. *"Keep An Open Mind."* "Don't impose your own narrative on the world all around you."

The Collectors
by David Baldacci
(New York: Hachette Book Group, 2006)

Key Insights:

1. *Keys to a Successful Mission.*
   a. Keep it simple;
   b. Provide for every contingency; and
   c. Do not panic when the plan goes awry, because a plan usually does at some point.

2. *On Collecting.* Everyone should collect *something*. It makes you feel more alive and connected to the world.

3. *Observation and Action.* "It was remarkable what could be accomplished when one was steadfastly observant and then acted on those observations with both courage and ingenuity."

4. *On Being Conned.* The best cons keep their mouths shut. "The best cons, you never knew they were there."

5. *Definition of a Good Life.* "Lives lived fully and the good deeds of past generations influencing the future ones."

6. *Details, Details, Details.* Never miss life's small details; they add up to avoiding mistakes or enhancing gains.

A Dangerous Fortune
by Ken Follett
(New York: Dell, 1993)

Key Insights:

1. *Don't Be Idle. The Bible* says, "If any would not work, neither should he eat."
2. *Banking Conservatism.* "Self-preservation was the highest duty of the banker."
3. *Out of the Public Eye.* Ordinary people can do many things without attracting attention. Public figures cannot.
4. *Investing Conservatism.* Invest only in good quality shares and avoid flashy speculation. Your judgment will be rewarded. "Where other men see profits, I see high risks, and I resist the temptation."
5. *No Exceptions Investing.* "The willingness to make exceptions" can deeply harm you in investing.
6. *Risk Sharing.* Minimizing risk is what banking is all about. A bank that can get a second bank to underwrite a loan gets less profit for itself but has less risk if the loan does not pay. It also gets additional targets for angry noteholders to chase.
7. *A Quicksand Investment* . . . is one that steadily pays dividends for years, but then the dividend and the investment evaporate.
8. *Integrity* is . . . telling the truth, keeping promises, and taking responsibility for mistakes.

A Regular Guy
by Mona Simpson
(New York: Vintage Books, 1996)

<u>Key Insights</u>:

1. *On Thinking Big.* "If a man wants the face of the earth to look different after his life upon it, he must think on a certain scale."

2. *Subtle Differences.* "The difference between the mediocre and the sublime was often a matter of proportion."

3. *The Midas Touch.* "In the last five years, he found himself in the odd circumstance of luck. Everything he touched turned to money . . . (He) probably experienced the strange apperception of momentum and the courage that came from it; his trajectory was going up and up, and if he multiplied the stakes, he could only multiply the gains."

4. *Skill Versus Luck.* "People always warned that in science, after you've made a great discovery, it's almost impossible to think the way you did before. And of course nobody believes it's luck when it happens to them."

5. *The Early Bird Gets the Worm.* "(He) liked being the first one up. Being awake at a time he usually slept made things feel important."

The Priest's Graveyard
by Ted Dekker
(New York: Center Street, 2011)

Key Insights:

1. *We Fear the Unknown.* "He was only staring at darkness, and darkness was often far more frightening than what it contained."

2. *On Morality.* There are two basic schools of moral thinking. One says an act is intrinsically wrong, regardless of the consequences, based on one's religion, law, or other code. The other says the consequences of the act must be factored into the moral assessment. For example, it would have been okay to lie to the Nazis in order to protect your children's lives if the Nazis were searching for them.

3. *On the Greatest Skill in Battle.* "The only skill more important than combat (is) preparedness. Surveillance. Intelligence. Positioning. These (are) nine-tenths of any victory. The rest (comes) down to flawless execution."

4. *Sins and Religions.* The great religions all condoned the great sins at one time or another. "Had not Rahab the prostitute been called a great woman of faith for lying to save God's servants? Had not Jesus taken a weapon in anger to whip the merchants out of the temple? Had not God blessed David with many wives and mistresses?"

5. *Faith, Religion, and Rules.* "Faith isn't about a list of rules and regulations, it's about love . . . Religious authorities made it too easy to feel good about following those rules, regardless of love, and to frown on people who didn't follow the rules."

6. *On Learning.* "Once you learn something, you can never convince your mind that you didn't learn it."

7. *On Chance.* "Our lives hang in the balance of unpredictable situations . . . one minute you're driving down the road whistling a tune, the next moment the car right in front of you spins out of control and crashes. How you prepare for those unpredictable occurrences determines whether you live or die. Always leave an empty lane to your right or left for escape."

The First Counsel
by Brad Meltzer
(New York: Warner Books, 2001)

Key Insights:

1. *On Unwanted Attention.* "The moment you hit the glare of publicity is the exact moment they burn your ass."

2. *Inner Toughness.* Tough people who are successful often turn their toughness inward on themselves and rip themselves apart. They are hardest on themselves.

3. *Political Gestures.* A politician will repeat your name and touch you physically on your arm, hand, or shoulder. They use these gestures to establish a level of intimacy with you and get you on their side.

4. *If a Job Doesn't Pay Well* . . . people are clearly there for another self-interested reason, such as access and influence to a source of power.

5. *Be Real.* "You're a real person. That's why people like you."

6. *Don't Talk.* Lawyers let silence drag out to get you to talk.

7. *Bigger Fish.* The first rule of the schoolyard applies to life—there is always someone bigger than you.

The Lost Constitution
by William Martin
(New York: Tom Doherty Associates, 2007)

Key Insights:

1. *Think First.* Study the world quietly, think before you speak, and think even harder before you act.
2. *Principles* . . . make the man.
3. *A Different Look at Love.* "Love is for the rich men and fools. Ignore women until you gain a reputation."
4. *Men Aren't Perfect.* "Men might not always be what God intended them to be but most were decent just the same."
5. *Why America Works.* "In America, we get up in the morning and go to work and solve our problems."
6. *Small Profits.* "If you can't buy cheap and sell dear, make a little profit anyway."
7. *On the Constitution's Choice of Words.* James Madison said, "Every word decides a question between liberty and power."
8. *Better to Be Free.* Benjamin Franklin said, "Any man who surrenders a little freedom for a little safety deserves neither the freedom nor the safety."
9. *On Apologies.* It is okay to apologize once, but do not apologize twice, for that is a sign of weakness.
10. *Money, Brains, and Ambition* . . . a tough combination to beat.

11. *Being Small.* "I'm a mouse under an elephant. If the elephant rolls over, I'll be crushed. If I'm smart, I can live a long time in his shadow."

12. *Guard Your Resources.* "Don't use all your resources at once. Husband them. Preserve them. Protect them. Because you never know what lies ahead."

13. *Following in the Footsteps of Greatness.* "The giants are dead and now the midgets are following."

The Brass Verdict
by Michael Connelly
(London: Orion Books, 2008)

Key Insights:

1. *Keep Your Mouth Shut.* "Most criminal defendants talk their way into prison . . . The best piece of advice I've ever given a client is to just keep your mouth shut. Talk to no one about your case, not even your own wife. You keep close counsel of yourself. You take the nickel (5th Amendment) and you live to fight another day."

2. *Live Your Belief.* "Act like you are innocent and you will be perceived as innocent. Finally, you will become innocent."

3. *Avoid the Rush.* People like the emotional rush of putting their life on the line—gamblers, criminals, investors. We

are programmed to enjoy the decisions to put things on the line—avoid that temptation.

The Ambler Warning
by Robert Ludlum
(New York: St. Martin's Press, 2005)

<u>Key Insights</u>:

1. *"You Gotta Go If You Wanna Know."* To be effective, you have to be on the ground and see what is happening.
2. *Human Stress Response.* There is a point when the human body's system of stress hormones depletes itself—excitement or fear gives out to numbness.
3. *Occam's Razor*—the simplest explanation for why something happened is usually the correct one.
4. *Patience.* Action in great things is also coupled with boredom, tedium, and plans that never work out. You have to play out many scenarios and bide your time to achieve victory.
5. *On Uncertainty.* Risk is quantifiable; uncertainty is not. Uncertainty is the great blind spot we all need to consider in our decisions. What is it that we do not (or cannot) know.
6. *The Double Bump.* Make investments in assets that could be valuable for more than one reason.
7. *The Focus of a Regime.* The more totalitarian a regime, the more inwardly focused it will be. The more open a regime, the more outwardly focused it will be.

Reckless
by Andrew Gross
(New York: Harper, 2010)

<u>Key Insights</u>:

1. *Staying the Course.* Sometimes you step into something and you have to see it through, even if it costs you people or your career.
2. *A Tale of Volatility.* ". . . not to mention the company's stock: a year ago it was over 80 . . . last Friday it closed at 12."
3. *An Executive's Connection.* The head of the firm left responsibilities to others, but he never lost his love for the trenches.
4. *What Goes Up . . .* A generation of Wall Street financiers grew up with the market only going up, up, and up. The market can go down or stay flat for a generation as well.
5. *Don't Be So Sure.* "People who believed too strongly in anything always made (him) nervous."

Robert Ludlum's The Bourne Sanction
by Eric Van Lustbader
(New York: Grand Central Publishing, 2008)

<u>Key Insights</u>:

1. *Efficiency.* "He possessed the preternatural stillness of properly harnessed energy. He made no move unless he needed to and then used only the amount of energy required, no more."
2. *Maintain Emotional Control.* "The person who loves is as easily manipulated as the person who hates."

3. *We See What We Want to See.* Human beings "have an infinite capacity for rationalizing reality to fit their personal ideas."

4. *On Ideology.* On one hand, an ideology is beneficial because it grounds us and provides a backbone of commitment. On the other hand, if the ideology is too rigid, it results in tunnel vision, because "anything that doesn't fit within your self-imposed limits is either ignored or destroyed."

5. *On Retreat.* When a victim gains the upper hand, exit the field as quickly as you can.

6. *Every Action Has a Reaction.* You tell someone something, they act on it, and then subsequent actions follow . . . Be careful in that a negative action can reverberate for a long time.

7. *A Prisoner's Sanctuary.* Smart prisoners find a place in their mind to go where it is safe no matter what is done to them.

8. *Good Art* . . . moves you between reality and an imagined dream world where anything is possible.

9. *A Central Tenet of Life* . . . is that reality cannot be controlled. It is too random and chaotic, and only a fool thinks he or she can completely control life.

More Twisted: Collected Stories, Volume II (New York: Pocket Books, 2006)

Key Insights:

1. *Luke 12:15.* "Beware! Be on your guard against greed of every kind, for even when someone has more than enough, his possessions do not give him life."

2. *The Rule of Thievery.* "The more modest the take, the more likely that weeks or months will pass before the victim discovers his loss, if indeed he ever does."

3. *A Wrench in the Plans.* "It is not often the plan itself that goes awry, but an entirely unforeseen occurrence that derails a venture."

4. *Sherlock Holmes* ... said, "Data, data, data ... you must fill your mind with every fact it is possible to retain." Some piece of obscure data can be the difference between success and failure.

5. *Two Kinds of Excitement.* There are two different forms of excitement: one is the excitement of winning with something on the line, and the other is the excitement with the process of doing something you love."

6. *Misery Doesn't Love Company.* "Other people losing money doesn't take the sting out of *you* losing money."

7. *On Smarts.* "Smart always beats out luck in the end."

8. *Details Matter.* "It's knowing everything about the game—even the little shit—that separates the men from the boys."

9. *Walk Away a Winner.* The thing that separates real gambling winners from novices is their consuming drive to walk away from the table with more money than they had when they started.

Vanished
by Joseph Finder
(New York: St. Martin's Press, 2009)

<u>Key Insights</u>:

1. *Foundations of Wealth.* Honore de Balzac said, "Behind every great fortune lies a great crime."

2. *Lessons on Money.* "We both know what it was like to have a lot of money . . . after we lost it . . . (he) became obsessed . . . with what we'd lost." Don't lose your fortune by putting it at risk, and don't obsess about money to the point it clouds your judgment.

3. *On Caution.* Nehru said, "Being cautious is the greatest risk of all." "Audentes fortuna juvat" is Latin for "fortune favors the brave."

4. *Sprezzatura*—an Italian word that means to make something difficult look easy.

5. *Ignore Idiots.* "Never let an asshole rent space in your head."

6. *Close Combat* . . . is always over in seconds, not the minutes portrayed in the movies.

7. *Coming Down* . . . after an adrenaline rush or highly stressful event, low-level anxiety and mild depression can set in.

8. *Don't Focus on the Food.* "Never go to a business breakfast without eating first." You will be too focused on relieving your hunger to be sharp.

9. *On Deception.* Goethe said, "We are never deceived; we deceive ourselves."

10. *Be Patient.* "You never want to let your emotion, your impatience, get in the way of an operation. It's always the times when you most want to rush to the finish line that you need to slow down, take stock, do it right."

Hell's Gate
by Stephen Frey
(New York: Atria Books, 2009)

Key Insights:

1. *The Devil's Share.* When you cut a deal with the devil, the devil always gets his piece of you in return.
2. *Wildland Firefighting.* A smoke jumper's life during a fire season is "long hours, terrible working conditions, intense physical challenges, little praise, and danger everywhere. Along with more camaraderie and self-satisfaction in a summer than most people experience in a lifetime."
3. *Staying Under the Radar.* "He liked flying under the radar, liked his place on the periphery. Especially when it came to money." Not even his banker knew his net worth.
4. *Always Learn.* "When you lose, don't lose the lesson."
5. *Always a Motive.* Actions are always preceded by a motive. To figure out why someone did something, find the motive.
6. *On Information Exchange.* Be a receiver, not a transmitter, of information.
7. *Greed.* Never try to squeeze more profit from an investment than it will warrant.
8. *Speak with Authority.* He didn't try to muscle his way into the center of every conversation . . . however, when he argued a case, he stepped strongly into a leading role."
9. *On Formality.* Being formal with someone is a way of showing him or her respect.

Carved in Bone
by Jefferson Bass
(New York: Harper, 2006)

Key Insights:

1. *Life Ain't Easy.* Garrison Keillor said, "Life is complicated, and not for the timid."

2. *On Sorrow and Joy.* In *The Prophet*, Kahlil Gibran said, "When you are joyous, look deep into your heart and you shall find it is only that which has given you sorrow that is giving you joy. When you are sorrowful, look again in your heart, and you shall see that in truth you are weeping for that which has been your delight . . . They are inseparable. Together they come, and when one sits alone with you at your board, remember that the other is asleep on your bed."

3. *Family Ties.* "Even when your back's to the wall—especially when your back's to the wall—your family'll stick by you. Thick or thin."

4. *Fighting through Adversity.* "He's had some big disappointments to reckon with, and you can never tell whether somebody's going to walk out of the valley of the shadow as a bigger person or a smaller one."

5. *We Each Change the World.* "I think we all leave an imprint on the world, and on the people we cross paths with, sometimes in ways we don't fully understand."

Buried Secrets
by Joseph Finder
(New York: St. Martin's Press, 2011)

<u>Key Insights</u>:

1. *The Gift of Fear.* Fear is a great warning signal, a useful instinct. It tells us we are in danger, and we need to listen to it and use it to our advantage.
2. *Memory and Our Sense of Smell.* "Neuroscientists tell us nothing brings back the past as quickly and powerfully as a smell . . . The olfactory nerve arouses something in the limbic center of your brain where you store long-term memories on your mental hard drive."
3. *Menschenkenner*—a rare type of person Sigmund Freud called a judge of good character.
4. *Be a Force of Good.* "In the Gospel of John it says, 'We know that we are children of God and the whole world is under the control of the evil one . . .' Maybe there's just . . . evil in the world . . ."
5. *Strategic Deception* . . . "in war or in espionage, is just another form of applied psychology. The thing is, you never actually deceive your target—you induce him to deceive himself. You reinforce beliefs he already has."
6. *Don't Bury the Truth.* Emile Zola said, "If you shut up the truth and bury it under the ground, it will grow, and gather to itself such explosive power that the day it bursts through it will blow up everything in its way."

Kane and Abel
by Jeffrey Archer
(New York: St. Martin's Press, 1979)

Key Insights:

1. *Bet on Skill, Not Luck.* "Better to lose with a wise man than win with a fool."
2. *An Old Polish Proverb*—"A guest in the house brings God into the house."
3. *Among God's Gifts* . . . "Presence is bestowed on very few."
4. *The Curse of the Wellborn.* "He began to realize that most people from backgrounds as privileged as his lacked any real incentive to compete, and that fiercer rivalry was to be found from boys who had not been born to his advantages. He even wondered if it was an advantage to be disadvantaged."
5. *On Keeping Score.* "He recorded every one of his imaginary purchases and sales, the good and the not-so-good . . . in a ledger."
6. *4 Keys to a Good Investment*:
    a. Low multiple of earnings,
    b. High growth rate,
    c. Strong asset backing, and
    d. Favorable trading forecast.
7. *Taking Profits Off the Table.* "Once a stock doubled in price, he would sell half of his holding, trading the stock he still held as a bonus."
8. *A Couple of Good Life Lessons*:
    a. Don't gamble when the odds are against you, and
    b. Walk away from a deal when you have reached your limit.

9. *Act Like You Belong.* "If you have to pay a bill, always make it look as if the amount is of no consequence. If it is, don't go to the restaurant again. Whatever you do, don't complain or look surprised—that was something . . . the rich had taught him."

10. *Inflationary Growth.* "The upward trend . . . was fueled by a large influx of borrowed money (and) could only result in inflation to the point of instability."

11. *Selling a Loser.* "You could lose your shirt if you dump all your stocks with the market in its present state." "I'll lose a lot more than my shirt if I hang onto them."

12. *Know Your Market.* "You can either serve a small group of rich people or a large group of poor people, but never both."

13. *America.* "This is the only country on earth where you can arrive with nothing and make something of yourself through hard work, regardless of your background."

14. *Get Off the Sidelines.* "Throughout his life, he had always taken the initiative, never been an onlooker."

The Second Opinion
by Michael Palmer
(New York: St. Martin's Press, 2009)

Key Insights:

1. *The Longevity Recipe.* Long life is a disciplined diet, exercise, and the right genetics.

2. *Live Like You're Dying.* You never know when your time will come.

3. *Asperger's Adaptations.* People with Asperger's Syndrome have to create neuropathways and then repeat the behaviors to learn them, while the rest of us innately

possess the pathways. They can also struggle with chaos, uncertainty, unexpected changes, and difficult social situations.

4. *On Billionaires*. "People like us don't get to where we are without stepping on a toe or two reinterpreting a law here or there."

Born to Die
by Lisa Jackson
(New York: Zebra Books, 2011)

<u>Key Insight</u>:

1. *The Small Rewards of Parenting*. "As she headed toward the kitchen to whip up (Campbell's Chicken Noodle Soup), she heard softly, 'Thanks, Mom,' and she exhaled a long breath and almost smiled, remembering why she'd had children in the first place."

CHAPTER 5:
HISTORY AND HISTORICAL FICTION

"History does not repeat itself, but it sometimes rhymes."

—Mark Twain

The Road to Monticello:
The Life and Mind of Thomas Jefferson
by Kevin Hayes
(New York: Oxford University Press, 2008)

Key Insights:

1. *Exercising the Mind.* Thomas Jefferson believed, "The pursuit of knowledge . . . required the same kind of personal discipline as the pursuit of physical fitness . . . The faculties of the mind . . . are strengthened and improved by exercise."

2. *Mind and Body.* Jefferson observed physical fitness complemented a sound mind. Having worked alongside an obese lawyer, he noted the man was intelligent but lacked the stamina to see things through to their conclusion.

3. *Multiple Studies.* "The carrying on several studies at a time is attended with advantage. Variety relieves the

mind, as well as the eye, palled with too long attention to a single object."

4. *Hospitality's Burden.* When his father died and Jefferson became head of the family and estate, he chose to shutter the estate and attend college, in part to continue his studies but also to escape the burdens of hosting family and friends. Jefferson chose to study in Williamsburg instead of travelling to England because he felt it more important to gain lifelong friendships at home rather than abroad.

5. *Jefferson the Writer.* Jefferson was much more a writer than an orator. He said nothing at the First Continental Congress but did scribe many of the key documents and worked well behind the scenes. The written word often trumped the spoken word in that age; oratory faded after a while but the well circulated memo lived on. Jefferson wrote a lot, and many of his works were not adopted—his ideas were many times rejected.

6. *Natural Rights and the Law.* Jefferson looked to natural rights as often as he could in formulating the law, such as "increase and multiply," "do no harm onto someone you would not want done onto you," and people are naturally born free and have free will to do what they choose. Jefferson liked it when several forces of nature converged to provide the same legal decision, and he viewed such convergence as "nature's hand" pointing the path.

7. *Economy of Thought.* Jefferson liked to write with efficiency, never using two words when one would do. His best works are very precise.

8. *A Self Divided.* "The whole of my life . . . has been a war with my natural tastes, feelings, and wishes. Domestic life and literary pursuits were my first and last inclinations,

circumstances and not my desires led me to the path I have tried."

9. *Intellectual Contributions.* While politics was his profession, Jefferson made contributions as an amateur scientist. The sciences as professions had not yet emerged, so it was possible to dabble as a hobbyist and produce new findings.

10. *Favorite Fables.* Jefferson thought holding your tongue was a valuable trait from Aesop's fable of the tongue. The fable of the miller who tried to please everyone and ended up instead losing his "ass" in the process was another favorite. And, the lesson of an old leader telling his sons that, if they act together no one can hurt them, but if they break apart and act alone, the world will tear them down.

11. *Meticulous Records.* Jefferson kept very detailed journals of his thoughts, musings, and purchases that were categorized by sections. He was also a stickler for accuracy and appreciated that trait in others.

12. *When Is Man Free?* "Telemachus (says) man is free only when fear and desire have no sway over him and when he is subject only to reason and the gods." Wealth also enabled a certain freedom, as espoused in "the well to-do gentleman whose opulence places him far above the perplexing pursuits and sordid cares, in which persons of inferior fortunes are usually engaged ..."

13. *On Legacies.* "A father lives on in the books he leaves to his son."

A Matter of Honor
by Jeffrey Archer
(New York: Pocket Books, 1987)

Key Insights:

1. *Money.* It is by far the most important commodity in the world. Everything else happens as a result of it.
2. *Impatience.* It is an excellent trait in business but terrible in poker.
3. *Playing the Odds.* "A banker never believes in going against the odds."
4. *On Value.* "As with all art, the value of an object can vary from one extreme to the other without any satisfactory explanation . . ."
5. *Keep Your Mouth Shut.* When being dressed down, or when you are uncertain of what someone else knows, remaining silent is your best option.

The Double Agents
by W.E.B. Griffin and William Butterworth
(G. P. Putnam's Sons, 2007)

Key Insights:

1. *Give Me the News.* "(Franklin) Roosevelt was the kind of man who knew he should hear bad news when that's what it was. He demanded to hear it—undiluted and never, ever withheld."
2. *Give Me the Best People.* Wild Bill Donovan was a Republican who opposed Roosevelt's New Deal, but Roosevelt did not care and wanted Donovan in the

Administration. Roosevelt liked Donovan's toughness, shrewdness, and character, which is what mattered.

3. *Calm, Cool, and Collected.* Roosevelt projected calm, even in the worst of crises.

Code to Zero
by Ken Follett
(New York: Signet, 2001)

Key Insights:

1. *Putting the Odds in Your Favor.* "A risky plan, but one with a good chance of success. In clandestine work, that's generally the best you can hope for."

2. *To Whom We Lie.* "When humans are under pressure, we're all willing to lie . . . We lie *more* to our loved ones, because we care about them so damn much. Why do you think we tell the truth to priests and shrinks and total strangers . . . It's because we don't love them, so we don't care what they think."

3. *How Did We End Up Here?* "Was he a weak man who had drifted into misfortune for lack of a purpose in life? Or did he have some crucial flaw in his character?"

4. *On Life's Big Choices.* "I decided, a long time ago, to sacrifice my personal life to something more important."

5. *A Good Speed. Festina Lente* is a Latin term that means "hurry slowly."

The Strange Death of Napoleon Bonaparte
by Jerry Labriola
(New York: Strong Books, 2007)

Key Insights:

1. *Never Give In.* Napoleon said, "In affairs of state one must never retreat, never retrace one's steps, never admit an error—that brings disrepute. When one makes a mistake, one must stick to it—that makes it right!"
2. *Some of Napoleon's Rules of War*:
    a. Avoid a field of battle the enemy has previously studied or reconnoitered.
    b. March dispersed but fight concentrated.
    c. Start the battle while holding back a large reserve. Decide on the enemy's weakest point and penetrate it at the proper time.
    d. Maintain unity of command.
    e. Avoid assault of a well-defended garrison.
3. *Napoleon's General Approach to Battle.* Napoleon liked a vague battle plan and then would adjust as the battle unfolded. Like a chess master, he was great at predicting his enemy's moves and then beating him to the punch.
4. *Napoleon's Successful Personal Habits*:
    a. Substantial capacity for work,
    b. High intellect,
    c. Phenomenal memory, and
    d. Courage.
5. *Napoleon's Fall.* Napoleon believed he could only be a great commander for six years due to war's physical deteriorations on a person. Napoleon repeatedly violated his rules of war after 1812, and many think he was drugged.

Fall of Giants
by Ken Follett
(New York: MacMillan, 2011)

Key Insights:

1. *Firm Convictions*. Lenin, Trotsky, and Stalin all had unshakable belief in what they were doing. Lenin also had an unbelievable capacity to outwork everyone else around him.

2. *On Aging Well*. "A wine cellar requires order, forethought, and good taste . . . the (same) virtues that made Britain great."

3. *Noblesse Oblige*. "War would be his chance to be useful, to prove his courage, to serve his country, to do something in return for the wealth and privilege that had been lavished on him all his life." "There were certain things you had to do before one could really call oneself a man, and fighting for king and country was among them."

4. *On Honor*. Shakespeare's Henry V said, "If it's a sin to covet honor, I am the most offending soul alive."

5. *An Apt Cliché*. "Pride comes before a fall."

6. *An Economy of Words*. "Never speak unless you have to."

7. *Storm Troop Tactics*. The Germans ignored the front lines and rushed to the back lines to sever communications. Infantry later mopped up the front lines once communications were destroyed.

8. *Unconditional Love*. "You don't love your family because they're kind and considerate. You love them because they're your family."

9. *Wartime Priorities*. "I joined the army to win battles, not promotions."

10. *The Fickleness of Public Opinion.* Politics isn't easy. No one said public opinion has to be consistent, right, or fair. Woodrow Wilson used public opinion like the wind—it blows the ship in a general direction, and a good politician can never head directly against it.
11. *In Conflict* . . . attack an enemy's weakest point.
12. *Treat Others with Consideration.* If you degrade others, sooner or later, it will come back to haunt you.

The Good German
by Joseph Kanon
(New York: Picador, 2006)

Key Insights:

1. *The Big Lie.* Nazi German's propaganda minister, Joseph Goebbels, said that if lie is big enough, nobody actually did it.
2. *Losing a Child.* "Do you know what it's like to lose a child? Both of you die. Nothing remains the same after that."

Eye of the Needle
by Ken Follett
(New York: HarperCollins, 1978)

Key Insights:

1. *Of World War II* . . . Winston Churchill said, "Never was so much owed by so many to so few."
2. *On Germany's Smartest Spy.* "If he had always obeyed his masters, he would not have survived so long." "Fear was never far from the surface of his emotions; perhaps that

was why he survived for so long." He was also a ruthless bastard who killed without remorse if anyone saw his face or knew his identity.

3. *Working with the Enemy.* Churchill hated Joseph Stalin with a passion, but he fought alongside him to defeat Germany in World War II.

The Revolutionary Paul Revere
by Paul Miller
(Nashville: Thomas Nelson, 2010)

Key Insights:

1. *Countries Can Get Tired.* On 17th Century England, John Winthrop observed, "This land grows weary of its inhabitants." Winthrop left England to lead a pack of Puritans to America.

2. *On Money.* "The love of money was the root of all evil ... the lack of it wasn't much better."

3. *On Taxes.* "Taxes play the villain in most any story of colonial America."

To Try Men's Souls: A Novel of George Washington and the Fight for American Freedom
by Newt Gingrich and William Forstchen
(New York: Thomas Dunne Books, 2009)

Key Insights:

1. *Our Pampered Life.* Since many soldiers were barefoot on winter marches, George Washington's men marched with the hope of getting a pair of shoes to wear in the snow.

2. *Out of a Population of 3 Million Americans* . . . a small group of dedicated people truly did change the world. George Washington had only 2,500 men with him to cross the Delaware River and sneak up on the British. "Thus it has always been. The labor is done by the few, and later many can lay claim to the bounty."

3. *Fire Washington?* As Washington lost battle after battle early in the war, Congress sent observers to report back on his success or failure.

4. *All Eyes on the Commander.* Washington "could not let the rank and file, standing but a few feet away, see him unnerved. Armies were the same throughout history. A commander's every word and gesture could . . . spread like wild fire to either hearten or create panic." "They will endure . . . cold and exhaustion for a chance at victory. They will not tolerate it if their leader is indecisive or confused. Certainty is the key . . ."

5. *Take a Chance.* "Prudence does not win battles . . . or wars."

6. *On What We Value.* "What we obtain too cheap, we esteem too lightly—dearness . . . gives everything its value."

7. *Words Matter.* Thomas Paine wrote beautiful, inspiring documents to keep the Revolution alive. Soldiers would lean over one another to read and hear his words of inspiration as they braved the elements and the enemy.

8. *A Tough Choice.* Washington wanted death with honor instead of surrender. If cornered, he planned to die by the gun.

The Barbary Pirates
by William Dietrich
(New York: HarperCollins, 2010)

Key Insights:

1. *A Small Military?* Thomas Jefferson, who argued against a large, standing military, found himself in the position of using five frigates commissioned by presidential predecessor, John Adams, to respond to pirates who threatened American shipping abroad.

2. *Fear of the Unknown.* "Horror we can habituate to. Defeat can be accommodated. It is the unknown that causes fear, and uncertainty that haunts us in the hollow of the night." "When the future is uncertain, the present is misery, and time creeps like a slug."

3. *On Wasteful Spending.* Benjamin Franklin said, "Buy what you have no need of and soon you will have to sell your necessaries."

4. *Meet on Your Terms.* Napoleon Bonaparte had "habit of seeing people on his own time and at his own advantage." He would wait to set an appointment with someone until they were dependent on his mercy.

5. *Personal Indications of Napoleon's Greatness.* Some of Napoleon's traits included: sleeping very little each night, maintaining an electrical presence, holding a firmness of command, and possessing a tense energy about him.

6. *The Ruler* . . . must always "bear the weight of rule."

7. *The Grass Is Always Greener.* "It's human nature to see the flaws in what you have and perfection in what you don't."

8. *On Time Management.* Benjamin Franklin said, "Most people don't sensibly fill the time they have already."
9. *Where We Spend Our Energy.* "Castles and cathedrals are where men put their energy . . . war and the afterlife."
10. *Humans in the Grand Scheme.* "Perhaps we're only a chapter in a longer tale. That we men are not the reason for existence, but just players in a bigger drama we don't understand."

Inca Gold
by Clive Cussler
(New York: Pocket Star Books, 1994)

Key Insights:

1. *The Pace of Progress.* Each project moves at its own pace. Some throw out the key answers with a shower of fireworks. Others become a series of dead ends and slowly die without a solution. You have to stick with your plan, because impatience or deviation from the plan can spell disaster.
2. *On Incentives.* "Motivation stimulated by incentive was a wonderful thing."
3. *Emotions.* "He would err again because his mind was clouded with hate and revenge."
4. *Manage Your Expectations.* "Hope for the best, expect the worst, and settle for anything in between."

Paths of Glory
by Jeffrey Archer
(New York: St. Martin's Press, 2009)

<u>Key Insights</u>:

1. *The Descent Is Always Harder Than the Climb* ... because of the energy expended on the way up means you have less for the way down, your climbing spots are at eye level on the way up but at your feet on the way down, and you can get complacent and relaxed after a successful ascent.

2. *Facing Death.* "Once you've stared death in the face, nothing is ever the same again . . . It places you apart from other men."

3. *Being Tested.* Only the very clever or stupid are sure of how they've done on a big exam.

4. *What We Remember.* Bertrand Russell observed that views formed from your home are always harder to dislodge than those taught in a classroom.

5. *On Defeat.* "When you know you're beaten, give in gracefully."

The Devil in the White City: Murder, Magic, and Madness at the Fair That Changed America
by Erik Larson
(New York: Vintage Books, 2003)

<u>Key Insights</u>:

1. *Think Big.* In 1893, Daniel Burnham, the Director of Works for the World's Columbian Exposition said, "Make no little plans; they have no magic to stir men's

blood." Burnham knew early in life he wanted to be more than just a home builder: "My idea is to work up a big business, to handle big things, deal with big business men, and to build up a big organization, for you can't handle big things unless you have an organization."

2. *When a Man's Work Is Finished*. Near the end of his life, Daniel Burnham commented, "This prolonging of a man's life doesn't interest me when he's done his work and has done it pretty well."

3. *A Commanding Presence*. Burnham possessed natural authority. "It was easy to see how he got commissions. His very bearing and looks were half the battle. He had only to assert the most commonplace thing and it sounded important and convincing."

4. *An Eye for Detail*. Burnham knew the tiniest details would shape how people perceived the World's Fair. For example, he focused intensely on the fair's seal, knowing it would be judged artistically as the fair's only exposure in many foreign countries.

5. *Form Versus Function*. Builders argue over form or function in a building's design . . . and they always will. Does the building take its shape around what is supposed to take place inside of it, or does the shape come first and only then dictate what type of work, hobby, or other activity should occur within it?

6. *Don't Quit*. Halfway through the World's Fair, Burnham wrote to his wife, "I presume anyone running a race has moments of half despair, along toward the end; but they must never be yielded to."

The Key to Rebecca
by Ken Follett
(New York: Signet, 1980)

<u>Key Insights</u>:

1. *Why Erwin Rommel Was Successful.*
   a. First, Rommel hated to retreat and believed one should always be on the offensive.
   b. Second, he wanted to be close to the battle so that he could make decisions based on first-hand information. He believed the British, on the other hand had it all wrong. He said, "The (British) generals are miles behind the lines . . ."
   c. Third, he was innovative on the battlefield and liked rapidly switching his forces, employing encircling movements, and surprising his enemy. "When they attack, I dodge; when they defend a position I go around that position; and when they retreat I chase them."
2. *A Leader's Energy.* Muhammad Anwar al-Sadat had "a burning idealism which gave him unlimited energy and boundless hope. Sadat was a senior member of Egypt's Free Officers Group that claimed power and installed Sadat as president of the country.
3. *Confining Defenses.* "The walls you build to protect you also close you in."

Thunderstruck
by Erik Larson
(New York: Crown Publishers, 2006)

Key Insights:

1. *Conjuring a Forgotten Past.* In the 1904 dedication to *Peter Pan*, J. M. Barrie observes, "A safe but sometimes chilly way of recalling the past is to force open a crammed drawer. If you are searching for anything in particular you don't find it, but something falls out at the back that is often more interesting."

2. *Inventor Versus Theoretician.* The inventor of wireless communications, Guglielmo Marconi, was not a theoretician and could not explain the physics behind why his wireless communications devices worked. "He gauged performance by instinct and accident." The scientists of his day looked down on Marconi as a mere inventor, but it was Marconi who made one of the world's all-time great discoveries.

3. *Humans and Communications.* "No matter how innovative the means of communication, men and women will find a way to make the messages sent as tedious as possible."

World Without End
by Ken Follett
(New York: Dutton, 2007)

Key Insights:

1. *Determination and Patience* ... are the two traits required to achieve any long-term goal.

2. *Know the Answer.* Never call a meeting unless the result is a foregone conclusion.

3. *Don't Think, Just Go.* "Pilgrims should not spend too much time planning their journey, for they might learn of so many hazards that they would decide not to go."

4. *Confidence in a Crisis.* In a crisis, people will follow the most assertive person if they seem to know what to do and possess a cool confidence.

5. *Work Bliss.* "He had the look of total concentration . . . This was what a man looked like . . . when he was doing what he was born to do. He was in a state like happiness, but more profound. He was fulfilling his destiny."

6. *On Leadership.* Most people worry about feeding their families. The natural leader worries about feeding the entire town.

7. *On Organization.* "The talent for organization is given to few people . . . when everyone else is baffled, or panicked, or terrified . . . I take charge."

8. *Hire Competence.* "Always do business with the most reliable supplier, always hire the best man for the job, regardless of friendship or family ties."

9. *Poor Man's Tactics.* "We who are poor have to use cunning to get what we want. Scruples are for the privileged."

10. *The Basis for Decisions.* Make decisions based on what you can see for yourself, not based on what some remote authority says.

11. *Hold Your Tongue Until the Right Moment.* Let a discussion run for a while so that when you propose your solution, people will be aware that there are no other alternatives, and they will be inclined to adopt what you propose. If you state your opinion right away, it will be natural for them to oppose it.

12. *One-Way Communications.* Many imaginative people talk to themselves.
13. *Logs and Lists* ... are keys to the organization, reflection, and discipline needed to achieve a goal.
14. *Rules* ... are there to protect you from yourself.
15. *Politics* ... over a long career will produce much more pragmatism than principle.
16. *Never Say, "I Told You So."* Instead, point out the facts and let the other side figure it out for themselves that you were right in the first place.
17. *The Good Leader* ... does not take the best for himself. He puts himself last.
18. *"What I Do Becomes Part of Me."* The spirit of divine retribution says that doing good makes you better and doing harm makes you worse.
19. *Know How to Make Money* ... and enjoy spending it too.

The Great Train Robbery
by Michael Crichton
(New York: HarperCollins, 1975)

Key Insights:

1. *Believing in the Future.* In the Victorian Age there was a grand belief in progress. "There was, in short, plenty of reason to believe that society was 'on the march,' that things were getting better, and that they would continue to get better into the indefinite future. The very idea of the future seemed more solid to the Victorians than we can comprehend. It was possible to lease a box in the Albert Hall for 999 years, and many citizens did so."

2. *Crime and Poverty.* The Great Train Robbery was shocking because Victorians thought crime would be eliminated as an inevitable consequence of society's progress. Crime was considered linked to poverty, plague, and other societal ills. The Great Train Robbery helped society see that criminal behavior would not fade away with societal progress and that its roots were not solely tied to society's ills. Regarding crime, we now know that "most offenses are committed through greed, not need." Criminals are also not of limited intellect, as was once commonly thought. Prison inmates' intelligences measure similar to the intelligences of the general population.

3. *Our Love/Hate Relationship with Crime.* "Our moral attitudes toward crime account for a peculiar ambivalence toward criminal behavior itself. On the one hand, it is feared, despised, and vociferously condemned. Yet it is also secretly admired, and we are always eager to hear the details of some outstanding criminal exploit."

4. *An Attitude of Respect.* "It is the demeanor which is respected among these people. They know the look of fear, and likewise its absence, and any man who is not afraid makes them afraid in turn."

5. *Greed and Ambition.* "The distinction between base avarice and honest ambition may be exceedingly fine."—Reverend Noel Blackwell, 1853

6. *Strange Institutional Bedfellows.* "The institutions of any society are interrelated, even those which appear to have completely opposite goals." Temperance societies and pubs, criminals and police, for example, thrive on each other.

7. *On a Well Planned Crime.* "Something can always go wrong."

The Given Day
by Dennis Lehane
(New York: William Morrow, 2008)

<u>Key Insights</u>:

1. *Pain Is Gain.* "Pleasure doesn't teach us anything but that pleasure is pleasurable. The nature of learning is pain. What molds us is what maims us. A high price . . . but . . . what we learn from that is priceless."

2. *Why Communism Failed.* "Communists . . . struck him as hopelessly naïve, pursuing a utopia that failed to take into consideration the most elemental characteristic of the human animal: covetousness. The Bolshies believed it could be cured like an illness, but . . . greed was an organ, like the heart, and to remove it would kill the host."

3. *America's Short Memory.* "This silly big country. You Americans—there is no history. There is only now. Now, now, now. I want this now. I want that now."

4. *On Slow, Steady Progress.* "Rome wasn't built in a day . . . But it was built."

5. *A Charmed Life.* "I wonder if you know how exceptional (it is) . . . to walk through this world without fear of other men . . . it suddenly embarrassed him that he'd moved through his entire life expecting it to work for him. And it usually had."

6. *How the Savvy Survive.* "An intelligent child born to less than advantageous surroundings . . . learns to charm . . . He learns to hide behind that charm so that no one ever sees what he's really thinking. Or feeling."

7. *A Priceless Possession.* "Your heart is purer than his . . . Don't ever sell that son. You can't buy it back in the same condition."

8. *What You See Is What You Get.* "There are only two types of men in this world—a man who is as he appears and the other kind. Which do you think I am?"

9. *Money Mastery.* "They ran the world . . . because they understood . . . money. They could predict its moment of passage from one hand to another. They also knew things . . . about books and art and the history of the earth. But money, most importantly—they had that down cold."

10. *When Time Slows Down . . . Or Speeds Up.* "There were times when violence or the threat of it slowed the world down, when everything came at you as if through water. But there were just as many times when violence moved faster than a clock could tick . . ."

11. *On Families.* "You can have two families in this life . . . the one you're born to and the one you build. Your first family is your blood family and you always (should) be true to that. That means something. But there's another family and that's the kind you go out and find. Maybe even by accident sometimes. And they're as much blood as your first family. Maybe more so, because they don't have to look out for you and they don't have to love you. They choose to."

12. *A Big Man.* "He was a giant . . . but he wore it lightly. Displays of vanity, after all, were the province of minor gods."

13. *More Than a Good Heart.* "You think because you've a good heart and a good cause that it'll be enough? Give me a fight against a man with a good heart any day . . . because that man doesn't see the angles."

14. *There Are Larger Forces at Play.* "Things had a way of working themselves out. So many men wasted so much valuable time and energy placing faith in the canard that they could control their destinies when, in fact, the world would continue to entangle and disentangle itself whether they were part of it or not."

15. *Don't Despair.* "Don't give in to the sin of despair ... It's the worst sin of all. God will help you through ... He just asks for strength."

16. *The Price of Family.* "The true price of family—being unable to stop the pains of those you love."

CHAPTER 6:
CULTURE

"If a man debauches himself, believing this will bring him happiness, then he errs from ignorance, not knowing what true happiness is."

—Socrates

Scratch Beginnings:
Me, $25, and the Search for the American Dream
by Adam Shepard
(New York: Harper, 2008)

Key Insights:

1. *The Goal*: Adam Shepard wanted to survive for 365 days, in a new town, with no connections, and without the benefit of his college degree. His goal was to start with nothing and end up with $2,500, a working car, a furnished apartment, and an opportunity to go to school or start his own business. In short, he wanted to prove that the American Dream was still alive—that you can start with nothing, climb the ladder, and succeed.

2. *Crisis Ministries*. Shepard started at a halfway shelter called "Crisis Ministries." The shelter worked because

it was temporary—residents knew they had to attend weekly review sessions towards goals they set, and they had to be on their own in a year. Shepard learned at Crisis Ministries that there are three types of people in life: those who make it happen, those who watch things happen, and those who sit back, scratch their heads, and wonder, 'What in the hell just happened?"

3. *Attitude Is the Difference.* Shepard talked his way into a moving company that was not hiring by stating he would work a day for free to prove himself.

4. *We Mirror Our Surroundings.* Shepard observed that hanging around the homeless led to a serious of bad behaviors and general decline in his bearing. He had to refocus himself to maintain a dignified appearance. He found it easy to slip into a creature of his surroundings if he was not careful.

5. *If You Keep Trying . . .* "The pendulum of life will swing your way." Les Brown famously said, "Shoot for the moon. Even if you miss, you'll land among the stars."

6. *Life Isn't Fair.* "The difference emerges among the people that accept that ideal (that life isn't fair), embrace it even, and bask in the unsung glory of knowing that each obstacle along the way only adds to the satisfaction in the end. Nothing great, after all, was ever accomplished by anyone sulking in his or her misery." Shepard observed, "Life is a bitch. Everybody faces adversity. Everybody. Nobody is immune. I met—and lived alongside—poor people in Charleston who were miserable and others who were delighted with their lives. By the same token, I've met millionaires who are some of the least happy people on the planet simply because they don't know how to handle their wealth, or worse, they have never

even had the opportunity to discover what happiness is in the first place. Adversity attacks at every level."

7. *America the Terrible.* "We live in an 'it ain't my fault' society. Nothing is ever our fault. Ever. We're fat because of our genetics, we suck at math because we had a bad teacher, and we're cheating on our wives because . . . It has nothing to do with the fact that we aren't eating right or exercising, that we aren't doing our homework, or that we aren't pulling our own weight in our marriages. It's everybody else's fault. It ain't ours."

8. *America the Beautiful.* "More than anything else over the course of my project, I grew to appreciate, even more than before, that we live in the greatest country in the world. America is more fertile and full of more opportunity than any country in the world. We are the eminent superpower of the planet. Can you imagine the results if I had done my project anywhere else in the world? You would think I would have had quite the success if I would have started in Asia or Eastern Europe or Latin America? You ever been to Guatemala? Wow. You want to talk about poor people with little opportunity? They live in huts, grow their own food, and drink unsanitary water. Their economy is so bad that they immigrate to Mexico in search of more favorable circumstances. So, in spite of all the whining and complaining that goes on in our country, I'd say we're doing all right."

9. *A Five-Year Plan* . . . "is invaluable. It gives us a sense of purpose in our present lives, the peace of mind every day that what we are doing has a purpose, a means to an end."

American Sketches: Great Leaders, Creative Thinkers, and Heroes of a Hurricane
by Walter Isaacson
(New York: Simon and Schuster, 2009)

Key Insights:

1. *People Make History.* Henry Kissinger said, "As a professor, I tended to think of history as run by impersonal forces, but when you see it in practice, you see the difference personalities make." *Time's* founder, Henry Luce always put a person on the cover instead of a topic or event, because he believed people convey lessons, values, and history. *The Bible* tells its most important stories, tales, and lessons through people.

2. *Creativity Makes All the Difference.* Walter Isaacson says creativity is what sets the most brilliant people apart from the rest of us. He says there are plenty of smart people out there, but the ones who can make a mental leap, see something different, and do something about it make all of the difference.

3. *Preaching and Storytelling.* Isaacson says there are two types of people from Louisiana—preachers and storytellers. The preacher tells you directly what the message is; the storyteller tells you indirectly. Know if you are a preacher or a storyteller. Sometimes, the story can have the greater impact. In *The Bible*, the stories resonate more than the lists of rules.

4. *Share the Credit.* Benjamin Franklin loved to come up with an idea and then deflect the credit to others. In doing so, he found his ideas were more easily adopted and that people ended up giving him even more credit for them in the end.

5. *Work with Others*. Franklin said, "The good men may do separately is small compared with what they may do collectively."

6. *Franklin's Take on Religion*. Franklin did not personally pray and believed more in doing good works here on earth. He proposed the daily prayer at the Constitutional Convention, not because he was religious, but because he thought it would bring the Convention attendees closer together and humble them. Franklin was a deist and did not want any single religion to dominate, so he gave money to all of the local religions. Franklin wanted to avoid one dogma being forced onto people.

7. *Franklin's Greatest Message* . . . was to transcend tribalism and embrace pluralism. At heart, he was not confident enough in his own judgment, so he kept an open mind. He believed more information and more opinions would lead to more truth.

8. *Conviction Versus Compromise*. Values can conflict with one another, and there is no magic formula that tells us when to compromise and when to stand firm. When he was Governor of California, for example, Ronald Reagan could be a hard-liner, but he also comprised when he oversaw abortion legislation, a state welfare bill, and a huge tax increase.

9. *When Should the United States Intervene Overseas?* Walter Isaacson believes the formula should be:
   a. When the crime is huge,
   b. When it is in a region that affects our stability, and
   c. Where there is an organization capable of dealing with the crisis.

10. *There Are Two Types of Leaders* . . . and society needs both kinds.

a. Build Consensus—Ben Franklin is a great example of consensus-oriented leadership that brings people together.

b. Defy Authority—Albert Einstein is a great example of a leader who defied authority. Einstein may have bucked authority, but in order to properly buck authority, you first have to be smart enough to know for what authority does and does not stand. Einstein could only challenge existing scientific thinking because he understood that thinking well enough to recognize its limitations.

11. *Love the Process.* Einstein loved the process of scientific discovery even when he failed, famously commenting, "The search for truth is more precious than its possession." He never lost his enthusiasm for discovery. Love the process of whatever you do, and you will never burn out.

12. *Two Keys to Success.* Bill Gates skipped his own classes at Harvard, attended other courses' lectures, and then crammed for his own classes' examinations. He believes that to succeed, you need to know how to make choices and think broadly.

13. *Democracy and Capitalism* . . . go hand-in-hand. China will be in trouble when its economic growth slows because its people are not truly free.

14. *The Disciplined Leader.* Gandhi gave us non-violence and non-confrontation as great underpinnings for our lives. In his disciplined commitment as a leader, he was strange. For example, Gandhi tested himself by sleeping naked next to young women.

15. *The Art of Getting Along.* George Plimpton shined in life because he always played the master of ceremonies.

He never strived to achieve anything, which made him lovable but also limited him.

What the Dog Saw
by Malcolm Gladwell
(New York: Little, Brown, and Company, 2009)

Key Insights:

1. *The Best Products Sell Themselves.* Ron Popeil, the inventor of kitchen gizmos made famous on late night television, would constantly ask himself how to make a home cook's job a little easier and then build his appliances accordingly. He had a relentless work ethic and would wake up late at night with flashes of inspiration that he would sketch on his night table. He never used a focus group, market research, or public relations team.

2. *What a Focus Group Will Never Tell You.* Humans do not always know what they want until they see it. For example, we never knew we wanted 30 different pasta sauce options until they were presented to us. Perfect is not always one platonic ideal; it sometimes comes in diversity, variety, and variability.

3. *The Human Palate.* There are five tastes on the human palate: salty, sweet, sour, bitter, and umami. Umami is the full-bodied taste of chicken soup, cheese, or milk. These five tastes are primal signals about the food we are eating, and they indicate, for example, calorie, amino acids, or protein density. Research shows Heinz Ketchup has no close competitors because it hits all five fundamental tastes at front, middle, and back of

the tongue. For this reason, we have no real variety in ketchups but many varieties of mustards. Brands such as Heinz and Coke offer a gestalt moment on our palate that cannot be replicated. These brands have no single distinguishing characteristic, such as a heavy sugar or garlic flavor, that we may enjoy once in a while but not every day. Other brands may be powerful on the palate, but we do not want to consume them every day.

4. *Avoid the Illusion of Progress.* Small risks become likely occurrences over long periods of time.

5. *On Heroes.* When society looks at its heroes, why just look at musicians, sports legends, politicians, or warriors? Why not look at Vidal Sassoon, who reshaped hair and a person's self-image? Look at people who used products to start a revolution, such as Steve Jobs or Bill Gates. What is a revolution if it is not accessible, tangible, and replicable?

6. *Defining Who We Are.* Our definition of ourselves is wrapped in bits and pieces, ideas and phrases, and rituals and products from the world around us.

7. *Your Conscience.* Keep your own conscience; never let anyone else keep it for you.

8. *Power Law Distributions* . . . look like hockey sticks when they are graphed. For example, Medicare's sickest 5 percent of patients account for 90 percent of its expenses and 5 percent of cars cause 55 percent of total car pollution. Use incentives to assist the outliers and most of the problem can be solved.

9. *A Fine Line Between Cheating and Creativity.* Cribbing, tweaking, and transforming something that already exists into something new is how music, literature, and products are created. What one calls cheating another calls the creative process. Nothing is created out of thin

air; it is always the extension of something that has gone before it.

10. *Complex Systems* . . . will periodically break down. What is clear in hindsight may not always be preventable beforehand. Models of complex systems should have normal accidents built into them that can be expected to occur over time. In fact, the zeal to correct a problem may set off unanticipated problems in the future.

11. *On Choking.* On the big stage, sometimes the side of our brain that controls explicit thought overrides the implicit side of our brain that allows us to function smoothly and effortlessly. People with a lot of experience behind them may less easily choke because they have more intuition to draw on that can override rigidity impulses. To avoid choking, we should relax and fight the urge to work harder.

12. *Risk Consumption.* Making something less risky might actually make it more risky, because people get more confident that they will succeed. For example, people get hit more in crosswalks than when crossing an open road because they feel safer in a crosswalk.

13. *Two Types of Genius.* Creative geniuses envision something and build it. They emerge early as prodigies. Work geniuses have to build something and tear it down until they get it right, and it may take them a lifetime to emerge because they do not exactly know what their end state is. The first type of genius is conceptual and the second type is experimental.

Ford County: Stories
by John Grisham
(New York: Bantam Books, 2009)

Key Insights:

1. *On Discipline.* "With practice, most unpleasant tasks become bearable."
2. *On Motivation.* A successful businessman made a habit of driving by his competitors' offices at 5 A.M. when he got to work, knowing that he had a daily leg up on them while they slept.
3. *Betting the Odds.* "He taught himself the discipline necessary to play the odds, to quit when he was losing ..." and to bet rationally when he knew the odds were in his favor.
4. *Three Attributes of a Professional Risk Taker:* (1) talent, (2) discipline, and (3) nerves.

The Nasty Bits
by Anthony Bordain
(New York: Bloomsbury, 2006)

Key Insights:

1. *Transformations through Travel.* "As you move through this life and this world you change things slightly, you leave marks behind, however small. And in return, life—and travel—leaves marks on you. Most of the time, those marks—on your body or on your heart—are beautiful. Often, though, they hurt."

2. *A Cook's Greatest Attribute* . . . is, "The ability to think fast, to adapt, to improvise when in danger 'of falling in the weeds' . . . even if a little corner-cutting is required."

3. *A Cook's Roots.* "Many of us yearn for those relatively carefree days when it was simply a matter of putting dirty plates into one end of a machine and then watching them emerge clean and perfect from the other end. Similarly, I have seen owners of multiunit restaurant empires blissfully sweeping the kitchen floor, temporarily enjoying a Zen-like state of calm, of focused, quantifiable toil far from the multitasking and responsibility of management hell."

4. *Quantity or Quality.* "It all comes down to the old dichotomy, the razor's edge of volume versus quality."

5. *A Higher Calling.* "Isn't a great chef's ultimate responsibility to change things for the better? To seduce, coerce, and induce people to eat better, try new things, experience joy, even enlightenment?"

6. *What Can't Be Taught.* "As I've said many times before, I can teach people to cook. I can't teach character." Anthony Bordain loves to work with immigrants in his kitchens; they never quit and do not mind doing the dirty work that has become so distasteful to many Americans.

7. *Actions Matter.* "We have, all of us, made careful observations of the hierarchy around us, wondered, in moments of extremis, why, for instance, the boss just bought himself a Porsche Turbo when yesterday he said that checks would be late this week—and sorry, but we need to cut overtime."

8. *Don't Forget Your Roots.* "As citizens of the world, we should know what came before. How we got here. Why we do things the way we do them. Where our food comes

from. We should know what it was like for our humble predecessors, sweating and struggling in unrefrigerated larders, unventilated kitchens, the septic madhouse and twisting, low-ceilinged subcellars of restaurants past. We should remember the way it felt, scraping potatoes onto a garbage-strewn floor, scrubbing grease-caked pots with cold water, bending to the will of crazed and increasingly parsimonious masters. And we should understand not just how much has changed, but how much has stayed the same . . ."

Battle Hymn of the Tiger Mother
by Amy Chua
(New York: The Penguin Press, 2011)

Key Insights:

1. *A Tale of Three Generations.*
    a. The immigrant generation starts off penniless in the United States. They work hard to become successful engineers, doctors, scientists, or business people. They pinch pennies, invest in real estate, do not drink much, and throw themselves into their children's education.
    b. The next generation is born in America and is high achieving, typically play an instrument, attend a great university, and wind up surpassing their parents in income. They will spend money, drink cocktails, and parent their children much less aggressively than the immigrant generation.
    c. The third generation is one of privilege and decline. They are much more likely to

disobey their parents and develop a sense of entitlement.

2. *Everyday Education.* Look up every word you do not know in the dictionary and memorize its definition.

3. *What Chinese Parents Understand.* Nothing worthwhile is fun until you are good at it. Mastering the basics is not fun and requires the fortitude of parents to force the children to master them.

4. *The Chinese Virtuous Cycle.* "Tenacious practice . . . is crucial for excellence . . . rote repetition is underrated in America. Once a child starts to excel at something . . . he or she gets praise, admiration, and satisfaction. This builds confidence and makes the once not-fun activity fun. This in turn makes it easier for the parent to get the child to work even more."

5. *Chinese Parenting Limitations: One Adult's Outcome.* "I always worried that law really wasn't my calling. I froze whenever a professor called on me. I also wasn't naturally skeptical and questioning; I just wanted to write down everything the professor said and memorize it."

6. *Building Self-Confidence.* "As a parent, one of the worst things you can do for your child's self-esteem is to let them give up. On the flip side, there's nothing better for building confidence than learning you can do something you thought you couldn't."

7. *Face Your Fears.* "Never not try something out of fear . . . Everything I've ever done that's valuable is something I was terrified to try."

8. *Make Your Own Luck.* Thomas Jefferson said, "I'm a huge believer in luck, and the harder I work the more I have of it."

Into the Wild
by Jon Krakauer
(New York: Anchor Books, 1996)

<u>Key Insights</u>:

1. *Alone with Nature.* "At long last he was unencumbered, emancipated from the stifling world of his parents and peers, a world of abstraction and security and material excess, a world in which he felt grievously cut off from the raw throb of existence."

2. *To Withdraw and Discover.* Paul Shepard, in his book, *Man in the Landscape* said, "To the desert go prophets and hermits; through deserts go pilgrims and exiles. Here the leaders of the great religions have sought the therapeutic and spiritual values of retreat, not to escape but to find reality."

3. *Are You Really Living?* "So many people live within unhappy circumstances and yet will not take the initiative to change their situation because they are conditioned to a life of security, conformity, and conservatism, all of which may appear to give one peace of mind, but in reality nothing is more damaging to the adventurous spirit within a man than a secure future. The very basic core of a man's living spirit is his passion for adventure."

4. *Love Is Everywhere.* "You are wrong if you think joy emanates only or principally from human relationships. God has placed it all around us. It is everything and anything we might experience. We have to have the courage to turn against our habitual lifestyle and engage in unconventional living."

5. *On Youthful Adventure.* "The older person does not realize the soul-flights of the adolescent." Adults forget the passions and longings of youth.

6. *On Risk.* "A challenge in which a successful outcome is assured isn't a challenge at all."

The New York Public Library's Books of the Century by Elizabeth Diefendorf (Oxford, England: Oxford University Press, 1997)

<u>Key Insights</u>:

1. *On Fighting Evil.* Mohandas Gandhi's "devotion to truth" philosophy had at its core to "always try to overcome evil by good, anger by love, untruth by untruth ... There is no other way of purging the world of evil."

2. *What's Real in Life?* William James believed in "life as it is experienced, not as it is theorized." On religious ecstasy, he believed, "it must be real. Although we cannot rationally locate its source, it is possible to affirm the effects of faith. From case studies of many religions, James concluded that 'we can experience union with something larger than ourselves and in that union find our greatest peace.'"

3. *The Courage to Be.* Paul Tillich offered as his "core message that 'courage was essential to the experience of meaning of life.' It was not merely one virtue among others, but the fundamental virtue upon which all others depend."

4. *Size Matters.* E. F. Schumacher said, "Man is small, and therefore, small is beautiful. To go for giantism is to go for self-destruction."

5. *On Science Fiction.* John Updike said, "Any futuristic novel . . . is about the present: what has struck the writer as significant and ominous in the world now."

6. *On Unity of Command.* When Winston Churchill became Prime Minister, he wrote, "I was conscious of a profound sense of relief. At last I had the authority to give directions over the entire scene."

7. *On Etiquette.* Emily Post said, "Etiquette is the science of living. It embodies everything. It is the code of sportsmanship and of honor. It is ethics."

8. *Plain Speaking.* Langston Hughes believed that a simple man speaking simple truths is always of value in a complicated and error-prone world.

The Imperfectionists
by Tom Rachman
(New York: Dial Press, 2010)

Key Insights:

1. *Ambition = Progress.* "Nothing in all civilization has been as productive as ludicrous ambition. Whatever its ills, nothing has created more. Cathedrals, sonatas, encyclopedias: love of God was not behind them, nor love of life. But the love of man to be worshipped by man." Grand motives do not produce great works; a grand hunger for status does.

2. *Standards . . .* are what set long term excellence apart from flashes in the pan. Hold to the standards.

3. *Witnessing a Lived Life.* "Now here he is, temples graying, eyes bagged, slightly handsome but slightly jowly, wearing the sleepy surrender of the family man."

4. *The Boss*. "It's strange to be the boss, knowing they discuss you, doubt you, resent you, and . . . complain, bitch, and moan about you."
5. *Motives*. "Everybody has motives. Name the person, the circumstances, I'll name the motive. Even saints have motives—to feel like saints, probably."
6. *On Larger Than Life People*. "Everyone felt this way about (him) . . . this amplified sense of their importance in his life. He had that effect. His attention had been a spotlight; all else dimmed."
7. *Watch the Press*! "Good reporting and good behavior are mutually exclusive."
8. *Revenge* is "better in principle than in practice . . . there's no real satisfaction in making someone else suffer because you have."
9. *Life As Bodies in Motion*. "When you encounter people, you and they have separate trajectories, each person pushing in a different direction."

I Am Charlotte Simmons
by Tom Wolfe
(New York: Farrar, Straus, and Giroux, 2004)

Key Insights:

1. *Cultural Para-Stimuli*. "A strong social or cultural atmosphere (even an abnormal one) could in time overwhelm the genetically determined responses of perfectly normal, healthy animals."
2. *When You Have More to Lose*. "The advantage the black players had was absolute determination to prevail in (the) game. To them it was a disgrace to let yourself be

pushed around by anybody and a terminal humiliation to let yourself be pushed around by a white player."

3. *Two Types of People.* In life there are those who cower and those who command. The vast majority of leaders from prior ages were warriors—a few were religious leaders—but most were warriors.

4. *Hush, Hush.* Men do not speak about most of life's true humiliations.

5. *On Time.* Only humans have a sense of time. In the cosmos, time is not real—matter simply keeps changing.

6. *Brains and Computers.* "Why is it the more a human brain knows, the faster it works, while the more a computer knows, the slower it works?"

7. *Shake Hands with Fortune.* "A loser's just like everybody else, except that he won't shake hands with good luck."

The Corrections
by Jonathan Franzen
(New York: Picador, 2001)

Key Insights:

1. *Don't Grab the Last Dollar.* "It seemed to her that in trying to save money in life, she had made many mistakes ..."

2. *Does Money Define Us?* "The problem was money and the indignities of life without it ... He wasn't covetous, he wasn't envious. But without money he was hardly a man."

3. *The Value of a Dollar.* "The old man's careful plucking of bills from his slender wallet and his faint hesitation

before he offered them were signs of his respect for a dollar ... of his belief that each one mattered."

4. *On a Profession.* A profession offers stability and order to life.

5. *Don't Be a Dabbler.* "It's usually best to choose one plan and stick with it."

The Man Who Made Lists
by Joshua Kendall
(New York: G. P. Putnam's Sons, 2008)

Key Insights:

1. *The Man Behind the Modern Thesaurus.* Peter Mark Roget developed the Roget's Thesaurus that helped generations develop better word choices to describe their world. As a child whose father died young and whose mother was overbearing, Roget buried himself in books to cope with sadness and anger. Roget had a hard time choosing words, so the development of a personal thesaurus grew out of personal need. Categorizing words and concepts brought him a sense of order that turned into an obsession. Obsessions, unlike other psychological issues, stay consistent over one's life span. Roget was a doctor who did not enjoy interacting with patients but stuck with the career because he felt it too hard to change jobs. Roget was driven to produce the thesaurus because he was anxious to make a contribution in life. He took opium to sleep at night.

2. *Good is Seldom Far from Evil.*

3. *Early Lumps.* Life's first disappointment is usually felt more severely than it ought to be.

The Beach
by Alex Garland
(New York: Riverhead Books, 1999)

Key Insights:

1. *Infinite Possibilities.* "If you accept that the universe is infinite, then that means there's an infinite amount of chances for things to happen . . . (and) if there's an infinite amount of chances for something to happen, then eventually it will happen—no matter how small the likelihood."

2. *Two Forms of Development.* Development can occur through evolution or it can occur through design.

3. *Universal Language.* The most widely understood word in the world is "Okay," followed by "Coke."

4. *How to Get Things Done.* "The way to get things done (is) to go ahead and do them. Don't talk about going to Borneo. Book a ticket, get a visa, pack a bag, and it just happens."

5. *Give.* Luke 6:38: "Give, and gifts will be given to you, for whatever measure you deal them out to others will be dealt to you in return."

6. *The Worst Case Is Better Than Uncertainty.* "Even if it was the worst-case scenario . . . at least the situation would become tangible. It would be something that was in our power to affect."

CHAPTER 7:
PHILOSOPHY, PSYCHOLOGY,
AND RELIGION

"The meaning of life is creative love. Not love as an inner feeling . . . but love as a dynamic power moving out into the world and doing something original."

—Ray Kurzweil

The Kazdin Method for Parenting the Defiant Child
by Alan Kazdin
(New York: Mariner Books, 2008)

Key Insights:

1. *Reward Versus Punishment.* Most parenting strategies over-emphasize discipline: "We concentrate so intensely on the behavior we want to eliminate that we forget to praise and reinforce the behavior we do want." B. F. Skinner, the father of behaviorism, said to never punish a child because there are too many side effects and unintended consequences. Rewards for small positive behaviors lead to better outcomes than do punishments for negative behaviors.

2. *The Downsides of Punishment*:
    a. It draws reinforcing attention to negative behavior.
    b. It increases hostility towards the parent from the child and towards the child from the parent.
3. *Rewiring the Brain.* If a child's short-term behavior can be changed on a repetitive basis, the brain rewires itself towards positive behavior instead of negative behavior. Chemical and structural changes occur through the repetitive practice of good behavior.
4. *Everyone Benefits from Better Behavior.* "Research shows that when a child's behavior improves, the parents' levels of depression, anxiety, and stress go down, and families get along better."
5. *Plenty of Advice . . . but Little Evidence.* There are over 300 child and adolescent therapy strategies, but only 10 percent of them have ever been successfully tested.
6. *Redefining the "Perfect" Child.* Even the most well behaved children listen only 80 percent of the time.
7. *Avoid "Caboosing."* Do not praise a behavior and then couple it with negative reinforcement. For example, "It's good you cleaned up your room . . . Why can't you do this every day?"
8. *Brains Mature Differently.* Calendar age is not a good measure of what a person can do. Different portions of the brain develop at different times, and those portions develop differently in each child.
9. *Charts.* Charting goals towards positive behavior has been proven to reinforce good behaviors. When identifying which goals to track, do not try to change everything at once. A system as complex as a child's behavior needs to be finessed a little at a time.

10. *Childhood Risk*. Research shows that children who never experiment with risky behavior in adolescence are just as, if not more than, at risk for aberrant adult behavior than those who experiment.

Fragments: The Collected Wisdom of Heraclitus **by Heraclitus and translated by Brooks Haxton (New York: Viking Press, 2001)**

Key Insights:

1. *"The Beginning is the End."*
2. *"Whatever You Say About Anything, Its Opposite Is Equally True."*
3. *"Declarations Will Always Be Self-Contradicting, Relative, Subjective."*
4. *Dreaming* . . . is "the frickering activity of the mind participating in the world's imagination."
5. *Comfortable, Complacent, Content*—"these soporifics extinguish the fire of the soul."
6. *The Unknown*. "Neither your hope nor your fantasies tell you anything about what comes after death. The unknown is not revealed by faith."
7. *"One's Bearing Shapes One's Fate."* "Fate is not governed from elsewhere, but is in your character, the way you bear yourself each day."
8. *The Prophet's Voice* . . . "requires no ornament, no sweetening of tone, but carries over a thousand years."
9. *Justice* . . . "keeps the book on hypocrites and liars."
10. *Emotional Control*. "To be evenminded is the greatest virtue."
11. *We Covet What We Miss*. Health is appreciated best after sickness, food after hunger.

American Gods
by Neil Gaiman
(New York: Perennial, 2003)

<u>Key Insights</u>:

1. *On Happiness.* "Call no man happy until he is dead."
2. *On Specialization.* "The kind of behavior that works in a specialized environment . . . can fail to work outside such an environment."
3. *On Gods.* "Gods die. And when they truly die they are unmourned and unremembered. Ideas are more difficult to kill than people, but they can be killed, in the end."
4. *The Foundations of Liberty.* "Liberty . . . is a bitch who must be bedded on a mattress of corpses."
5. *A Feel-Good Guy.* "The old security guard was gruff, earnest—a little bumbling perhaps, but enormously well-meaning. Everyone who gave him their money walked away a little happier from having met him."
6. *A Theory on Why Gods Used to Speak Directly to Us.* Approximately 5,000 years ago the right and left lobes of the brain fused. Prior to that fusion, when the right lobe of the brain said anything, it was perceived as a voice from some other being.
7. *What Do We Worship?* We worship the television, video games, or computers by giving them time and attention over other things in our lives.
8. *On Moral Certainty.* The biggest wars are fought by people who believe they are right without a doubt.
9. *The Gambler's Rush.* People gamble to lose money; they make a sacrifice in exchange for feeling alive, to be able to lose themselves for a while in a game.

10. *Be Careful What You Wish For.* "Spells sent to hurt (another) will only hurt the sender." Make love, not anger or fear, be what drives you.

11. *On Survival.* "You only get to my age by assuming the worst."

Sign of the Cross
by Chris Kuzneski
(New York: Jove Books, 2006)

Key Insights:

1. *"Knowledge Is the Enemy of Faith"*—Stone marker inscription, 37 A.D.

2. *On Enemies.* "All organizations—even the innocuous ones—have enemies. No matter what you do, whether it's good or bad, someone's bound to be offended."

3. *Bad Religion.* Religion was started as a means for the elite to control the masses. "He who possesses the ear of God is a very powerful man." It is one thing to threaten man with punishment; it is another to threaten eternal damnation. Controlling people is not permanent, for the world has a way of changing over time.

The Lost Symbol
by Dan Brown
(New York: Anchor Books, 2009)

Key Insights:

1. *Religions and Masons.* Religions assure salvation, believe in a specific theology, and convert non-believers. Masons do not promise salvation, have no specific ideology,

and do not attempt to convert anyone. In fact, within Masonic lodges, discussions of religion are prohibited. Masons do not recruit members, nor do they respond to their critics.

2. *Masonic Death Symbolism.* Masons use symbols of death to inspire themselves to lead better lives while on Earth. A famous Mason, Benjamin Franklin said, "More leaders should ponder the finality of death before racing off to war."

3. *Thinking Changes Reality.* Our thoughts actually have mass. They exert gravity and can pull things to them. Recent experiments have proven that human thought has the ability to affect and change critical mass. "Our thoughts actually interact with the physical world, whether we know it or not, effecting change all the way down to the subatomic realm." "If thoughts affect the world, then we must be very careful how we think. Destructive thoughts have influence, too, and we know it's far easier to destroy than it is to create." Some people are better at using their thoughts to affect change than others; the ability can also be enhanced through practice. The power of human thought also grows exponentially with the number of minds that share the thought. Two heads are literally better than one.

4. *The Principle of Noetic Science.* Living consciousness is the influence that turns the possibility of something happening into something really happening.

5. *Advances in Knowledge.* "Knowledge grows exponentially. The more we know, the greater our ability to learn, and the faster we expand our knowledge base . . . mathematically speaking, as time passes, the exponential curve of progress becomes almost vertical, and new development occurs incredibly fast."

6. *On God.* God is within us. "A wise man once told me ... the only difference between you and God is that you have forgotten you are divine." "The second coming is the coming of man—the moment when mankind finally builds the temple of his mind." Revelations and the apocalypse actually predict an age of great wisdom, not the stories that we have been taught. It was our minds that were created in the image of God, not our bodies. We all have the story of truth in our DNA. If we all gravitate to the same ideas, maybe we are not learning them but instead recalling them because they are already part of our consciousness at some level.

7. *Living for Others.* The famous Mason, Albert Pike said, "What we have done for ourselves alone dies with us; what we have done for others and the world remains and is immortal."

8. *Compassion and Forgiveness* ... are so hard to give but they are the best thing to do.

The Big Questions: Tackling the Problems of Philosophy with Ideas from Mathematics, Economics, and Physics by Steven Landsburg (New York: Free Press, 2009)

Key Insights:

1. *Which Is a Better World?* Would you prefer one billion VERY happy people or 10 billion SOMEWHAT happy people? Your answer depends on whether you prefer to maximize total happiness or average happiness.

2. *Marital Division of Labor.* John Kenneth Galbraith explained of his family's division of labor: he settled the big issues and his wife settled the small ones.

3. *On the Universe.* Steven Landsburg believes the universe exists for a reason, but we have not yet uncovered what that reason is.

4. *On Economists' Predictions.* Scott Adams said that economists are generally "wrong with complicated models but right about concepts ..." By way of analogy, a mechanic knows that changing your oil is good for your car's engine, but he cannot tell you precisely when the engine will break down if you fail to change the oil.

5. *Good Economic Models* ... can be verified mathematically and then recast as stories that people can understand.

6. *Natural Selection* ... operates at the genetic, not at the organism, level. Genes prosper when they have effective survival and reproduction strategies, which is why humans are willing to die to save others, for example.

7. *Costless Beliefs.* Steven Landsburg states that people cling to beliefs that do not matter in their everyday lives. For example, people will believe passionately in religious faith that they cannot prove because it does not hurt them in their everyday life if they do. If someone is hurting them because of their faith, many people will then reexamine that faith and deny it. Landsburg believes, "When it's important to get things right, we replace our beliefs with knowledge." "If you're going to survive in this world you've got to pick and choose what you're going to think hard about."

8. *Repeating Your Fallacies.* The beliefs we go around repeating are the ones we really do not believe. For example, we believe 2 + 2 = 4, so we do not constantly revisit the matter.

9. *What We Really Care About* ... are the issues about which we spend our time thinking, meditating, and reflecting.

10. *Two Sources of Cognition.* Cognition comes from two different parts of the brain. One part deals with causality in the physical world, and the other part deals with understanding the social world. For example, if a gun is fired, our brain understands that the gun fired because someone pulled its trigger (i.e., the physical world understanding) and because someone was angry that her spouse was cheating (i.e., the social world understanding). The two sides of the brain evolved at different times, with the side dealing with the physical world having evolved much earlier. It is the physical side that is shared with other animals.

11. *Inflated Sense of Self.* We place too much stock in our own opinions. To admit we are stupid would be counter to evolutionary survival.

12. *Philosophical Rules of Thumb.* Do not leave the world worse off than you found it, do not spend time and energy on nonproductive societal behaviors, and do not be envious of others.

13. *Economists* ... measure all costs and benefits of the world as a system, not as a measurement of any particular individual within the system. So, an economist would view someone who lost a job as someone who has still benefited from living standards that have improved in the economy over their lifetime. When you see the world as an economist, you can lose track of seeing it through the eyes of a normal person.

14. *Random Economic Observations.* Internet pornography has reduced rapes in the United States by 7.3 percent annually; one inch of additional height produces $1,000 in additional annual wages; it is okay to lose an argument because you have learned something in the process and thus made yourself more valuable; and no one "would

want to be judged by the most foolish thing he'd ever said in print."

Triumph: The Power and the Glory of the Catholic Church: A 2,000-Year History
by H. W. Crocker III
(Roseville, California: Prima, 2001)

Key Insights:

1. *Size.* The Catholic Church has over one billion members and is the world's largest organized religion.

2. *Standing on Principle.* In *Death of a Gentleman*, Christopher Hollis says, "The principles are settled. Life is . . . men and women living up to them or failing to live up to them . . . If we are to save ourselves, we need to close our minds, to take honor's worth for granted and to escape back into certainty from the atmosphere of clerical questioning."

3. *Religious Freedom* . . . far outlives the American idea that it started here. Constantine's *Edict of Milan* provided religious freedom 1,400 years before America's version of it.

4. *On Authority.* Jesus "taught as one having authority, and not as the scribes." He broke new ground and was not simply interpreting or preaching what was already known.

5. *The Early Church's Roles*:
   a. Apostolic—it spread the gospel.
   b. Authority—its authority was grounded in an historical event witnessed by many people, which is a key feature that distinguishes it from other religions.

    c.   Hierarchy—Jesus created Apostles and they appointed Bishops to govern the Church.

    d.   Doctrine—scripture was not enough; the Church provided guidance on how to implement scripture.

6. *The New Testament* ... "was assembled to serve a Church already functioning and growing." Oral tradition provided the Church's teachings well prior to formation of the New Testament.

7. *Paul's Contributions*:

    a.   Salvation was available to all people, not just Jews.

    b.   Jewish law was no longer binding; nothing could separate the faithful from their God; not even the law.

    c.   There are three gifts—faith, hope, and charity—and the greatest of these is charity.

    d.   Paul, like Jesus, ignored politics. Both were loyal subjects of Rome and taught followers to obey Roman laws. The later Church avoided being subservient to the State, which cannot be said of all religions.

    e.   Through his letters that warn against errant ways, Paul gave the early Church a uniform system of belief.

8. *Heresy* ... has been around since the Church's earliest days, and it takes many forms, to include those claiming to be "holier" than the Church expects of its followers.

9. *Core Contradictions*. At its core, the Church holds extraordinary claims and intense realism at the same time. No one reasons himself into Christianity; it is a revealed religion that requires acceptance of the revelation of God.

10. *Opus Dei*—"To work is to pray."
11. *A Universal Church*. The Church expects its people to have faults and require forgiveness. Catholics are not charged to be brilliant; they are charged to be faithful and to maintain their fidelity to the Church.
12. *On the Dark Ages*. As Church leaders, the Dark Ages Popes had many failings and reflected their times, but they did manage to "keep the light of faith on" when the western world collapsed into barbarism and warfare.
13. *Protestantism* ... has many fissures and has at times been derogatorily referred to as, "Design your own religion."
14. *The Talmud* ... says, "Whosoever preserves one life, it is accounted ... as if he ... preserved the world."
15. *To Attack Is to Respect*. The best backhanded compliment the Church is offered is the notion that no one takes issue with other denominations or religions on issues such as who stood up and who did not stand up to the Nazis, for example. Only the Catholic Church is answerable to the rest of humanity for what it does and does not do.
16. *On Good Ideas*. Father Jerry Popieluszko said, "Violence is a sign of weakness ... An idea that needs rifles to survive dies of its own accord ... An idea capable of life wins without effort and is then followed by millions of people."

The Mystical Life of Jesus: An Uncommon Perspective on the Life of Christ
by Sylvia Browne
(New York: Penguin Group, 2006)

Key Insights:

1. *On the Truth.* The truth will make you free, but *you have to accept the truth* for it to make you free.
2. *Christ's Family.* Jesus came from a well-to-do, not a poor family.
3. *Christ the Communicator.* Jesus learned to communicate on the level of his audience; he spoke in stories and parables instead of dogma so people could understand and apply his teachings. He also used examples that are timeless.
4. *The Burden of Leadership* . . . was always on Jesus' shoulders.
5. *The Pursuit of Destiny.* Jesus knew he had a destiny, which is what drove him to travel, study different cultures, learn how to heal from India and the Far East, and absorb the philosophy of non-violence. He spent 15 years traveling and studying what others believed and may have picked up his healing powers through suggestive mind techniques and medical knowledge in India.
6. *"Seek and ye shall find* . . . "Jesus was a free thinker and encouraged the same of his followers. He readily incorporated many religions and beliefs into his own teachings. He led and encouraged a life of constant learning.
7. *Reverse Psychology.* Jesus told people not to tell of his healing powers, which of course had the reverse effect of

people talking about them. Jesus was humble, because he knew his powers came from God and were thus not his own.

8. *Working the System.* Jesus did not directly confront the existing systems of Rome or the Jews; instead, he was savvy enough to work within the systems as much as he could to get his message out, even though he knew much of prevailing Jewish health and other practices were bunk. Some think he needed a dramatic exit through a fake resurrection to get his message out, and that he lived out the rest of his life somewhere in Europe.

9. *A Universal Message.* Jesus' teachings were universal and transcended culture. The main message was to quit worrying about material things and focus instead on how you treat and love people. What you give out, you get back in return. He who is greatest shall be your servant.

10. *The Early Church's Portrayal of Jesus.* Some people think the Early Church had to compete among other neighboring religions and thus had to infuse some falsehoods in order to survive long enough to carry its message. The Early Church had to infuse false miracles, did not want us to see Jesus' humanity, and thus stripped references to experiences such as Jesus seeking knowledge or his relationship with Mary Magdalene.

11. *God.* The God of Jesus is all loving, not wrathful. Jesus thought evil deeds would come back to people who acted evil, not by a judgmental God. Some think he learned of karma in India. Jesus did not preach guilt, judgment, or evil; the early Church foisted those issues on humanity and made money on those fears.

12. *On Dying for Our Sins.* It was Paul, who never met Jesus, who said Jesus died for our sins. Jesus came to teach,

heal, and set an example. He did not come to impose a set of dogma.

The Man Nobody Knows: The Modern Life of Jesus Christ by Bruce Barton (Charter, 1962)

<u>Key Insights</u>:

1. *The Real Jesus*. Jesus was not a denier like John the Baptist who purged himself. Jesus had fun, liked to dine out, and enjoyed his friends. He loved his life, which is why he did not want to leave it. He was not the weak man so often portrayed today. Jesus was physically rugged from living outdoors and practicing carpentry for a living.

2. *On Petty Slights*. Jesus never let slights slow him down and neither should we. He was also patient with people who had a hard time grasping his vision. "No man can expect to accomplish anything if he stands in terror of public opinion."

3. *Follow Your Dreams*. Jesus did not want the sure thing of a carpenter's life; instead, he took a chance and had to find words to deliver his message in a way that everyone could understand. His consuming sincerity in his dream drew others to him like a magnet.

4. *A Self Divided*. Most of us go through life divided against ourselves as we manage families, jobs, investments, retirements, health care, and the rest of life. Jesus was not divided. There is a certain genius in being able to become a child at heart in adulthood.

5. *Time Management.* Although he was very busy, Jesus was never too busy to help people. He was accessible, but he also liked quiet time alone.

6. *Vision.* John the Baptist condemned what was wrong with then contemporary teachings, but he could not construct a vision. Jesus constructed an alternative vision to the status quo.

7. *Recruit and Inspire.* Jesus saw talents in men they did not know they possessed.

8. *A Great Debater.* Jesus was persuasive and skilled in debate; he had to constantly defend himself and his message.

9. *Be Unconventional.* Jesus did not follow conventions and rules.

10. *Humor.* Abraham Lincoln told jokes and laughed during the Civil War's darkest days. It helped him from going crazy.

11. *Why Christianity Survived and Still Works.* Christianity survived among many other regional religions because it maintains as core principles justice, goodness, and a singular God whom every individual may directly access.

12. *The Prophet's Dilemma.* People close to any hero are mystified by how the public adores him or her. Most prophets are not accepted in their own countries.

CHAPTER 8:
POLITICAL SCIENCE
AND POLITICAL FICTION

"Capture the right building at the right moment, and you
can take possession of an entire country."

—Matthew Lynn

In the President's Secret Service
by Ronald Kessler
(New York: Three Rivers Press, 2009)

Key Insights:

1. *The Leader's Ego.* "Even if an individual is balanced,
   once someone becomes president, how does one solve
   the conundrum of staying real and somewhat humbled
   when one is surrounded by the most powerful office in
   the land, and from becoming overwhelmed by an at times
   pathological environment that treats you every day as an
   emperor? Here is where the strength of character of the
   person, not his past accomplishments, will determine
   whether his presidency ends in accomplishment or
   failure."

2. *Appreciating the Plight of the Poor.* Ronald Reagan grew up poor, and as president, he wrote personal checks when he heard of poor children struggling. These checks were in amounts of $4,000-5,000 apiece. Reagan would tell the deliverer of the check not to tell anyone who wrote it.

3. *Think Beyond Yourself.* George and Barbara Bush were able to "think outside their own little world. They think of other people."

Jackdaws
by Ken Follett
(New York: Penguin Books, 2001)

Key Insights:

1. *The Flexible Response Defense.* "Rommel did not have enough men to guard the hundreds of miles of vulnerable coastline, so he adopted a daring strategy of flexible response: his battalions were miles inland, ready to be swiftly deployed wherever needed."

2. *Be Bold.* "Rommel had always favored the sudden bold assault over the cautious planned advance."

3. *The Best Laid Plans . . .* Battles never go according to plan; the smallest of mistakes can tip the balance to defeat instead of victory.

4. *Verbal Experimentation.* Sometimes it is good to try out ideas by throwing them out in conversation, rather than stating them with firm conviction—a verbal test of an idea without holding it as truth.

5. *Hard Thinking.* "You think of everything." "Yes, that's why I'm still alive."

6. *On Torture.* "The best torturers were men . . . who loathed the process from the bottom of their hearts." People

who enjoyed hurting others focused too much on the pain, and were ineffective. The objective is getting the information, not inflicting the pain.

Moscow Rules
(New York: G. P. Putnam's Sons, 2008)

<u>Key Insights</u>:

1. *Efficiency in Victory*. Don't play your ace when a jack will do the trick.
2. *On Taking a Loss*. It is sometimes necessary to take a small defeat in order to gain an ultimate victory.
3. *A Good Spy* . . . has unlimited patience, to hold his tongue, to wait for things to develop.
4. *Don't Wish for Adventure*. In the spy world boring is not always bad; it is the exciting, heroic deeds that can lead to death.
5. *Behaviors of the Idle*. Idle men tend to keep a strict daily regimen.

Broker, Trader, Lawyer, Spy:
The Secret World of Corporate Espionage
by Eamon Javers
(New York: HarperCollins, 2010)

<u>Key Insights</u>:

1. *It's Not All in the Genes*. "Sons don't bear the sins of their fathers, it's true. But history teaches that sons don't always bear their virtues, either."
2. *The Old Special Boat Service Motto*. "Not by strength, by guile."

Michael J. Hillyard

**Seeing Like a State: How Certain Schemes to Improve the
Human Condition Have Failed
by James Scott
(New Haven: Yale University Press, 1998)**

Key Insights:

1. *The Glue That Binds Production.* "Any production process depends on a host of informal practices and improvisations that could never be codified," which is why certain workplace rules and regulations make it so difficult to produce anything.
2. *Losing Culture.* "Global capitalism is perhaps the most powerful force for homogenization."
3. *On Complex Systems.* Isolating a single element in a complex system can have dire unintended consequences. For example, harvesting trees for lumber and thinking they can be replaced by seeding eliminates the forest's biodiversity.
4. *An Example of Diversity's Importance.* "A merchant who, not knowing what conditions her ships will face at sea, sends out scores of vessels with different designs, weights, sails, and navigational aids stands a better chance of having much of her fleet make it to port, while a merchant who stakes everything on a single ship design and size runs a higher risk of losing everything."

Bust: Greece, the Euro, and the Sovereign Debt Crisis
by Matthew Lynn
(New Jersey: John Wiley and Sons, 2011)

<u>Key Insights</u>:

1. *Institutions As Evolutionary Creatures.* "The natural impulse of any organism is to survive, replicate itself, and enlarge its territory."
2. *The Psychology of Money.* "Money is just paper with some colored ink and some solemn-sounding pledges printed on it. People have to believe it is worth something for it to have any value."

The Ghost War
by Alex Berenson
(New York: The Penguin Group, 2008)

<u>Key Insights</u>:

1. *The Great Man Theory.* "I'm not a fan of the great-man theory of history. The Confederacy had all the best generals and still lost the war."
2. *Servant-Leadership.* "He had the chauffeurs, guards, housekeepers. Still he always tried to remember that he served the people, not the other way around. Unlike other leaders, he hadn't used his position to make a fortune from bribes or corrupt business deals."
3. *Mao's Unintended Lesson.* "All nine (of the Chinese Standing Committee Members) had learned the same lesson that the Cultural Revolution taught everyone in China—though the lesson wasn't the one Mao had hoped to teach. Or maybe it was. Take what you can,

while you can. Because no matter how secure you think you are, you'll lose everything if the Party turns on you."

4. *Pigs Get Slaughtered.* "It's the fat pig that feels the butcher's knife."

5. *On Coincidence.* "Too many coincidences too soon. Nothing definitive, but if he waited for definitive he'd wind up in a cell or a wooden box."

6. *On Friends.* "A man should choose a friend who is better than himself."

7. *Don't Forget Your People.* "Dynasties crumble when emperors forget their subjects."

The Next Decade: Where We've Been . . . and Where We're Going
by George Friedman
(New York: Doubleday, 2011)

Key Insights:

1. *What Did Lincoln, FDR, and Reagan Have in Common?* All three men were presidents who defined greatness, "each of whom was a profoundly moral man . . . who was prepared to lie, violate the law, and betray principle in order to achieve ends." Strong presidents also create a fabric of illusions to do what is necessary without alarming the public.

2. *On Power.* "Power is only possible from a degree of ruthlessness most of us can't abide."

3. *On the Short—Versus Long-Term.* "In the course of a century, so many individual decisions are made that no single one of them is ever critical." Individual decisions matter much more over the course of a decade.

4. *Empires Don't Pop Up Overnight.* Lasting empires grow organically and their imperial status can remain low-key until it becomes overwhelming. The United States, Great Britain, and Rome were all unplanned in this manner. Napoleon, Hitler, and the Soviet Union were very much planned empires and did not last.

5. *Machiavellian Insights*:

   a. Good comes from the ruthless pursuit of power, not from trying to do good. "A man who wants to act virtuously in every way . . . comes to grief among so many who are not virtuous." Conventional virtues of a good person are not acceptable in a president who must exercise power. A president must be coldly calculating in staying focused on long-term objectives.

6. *On Economic Crashes.* "Every business cycle ends in a crash, and one sector usually leads the way."

7. *The Myth of Presidential Economic Control.* Presidents really have little control over the economy. Their job is to inspire confidence and sell a plan.

8. *The Impact of a Recession.* In the Great Depression, Gross Domestic Product fell by 50 percent. In contrast, during the 2008 financial crisis, Gross Domestic Product fell only four percent.

9. *"Nations Are Built in Blood."* Nations do not succeed when they are merely lines drawn on a map by a treaty or coalition. Nations grow on the roots of a shared history, sacrifice, legends, and overcoming odds.

10. *The Strengths and Weaknesses of Markets.* "Markets are superb at exploiting existing science and early technology, but they are not nearly as good in basic research." In contrast, "the government is inefficient,

but that inefficiency and the ability to absorb the cost of inefficiency are at the heart of basic research."

Game Change: Obama and the Clintons, McCain and Palin, and the Race of a Lifetime by John Heilemann and Mark Halperin (New York: HarperCollins, 2010)

<u>Key Insights</u>:

1. *Obama's 2008 Campaign Approach.* "Never too high, never too low." Obama's attitude was to avoid worrying about things out of his control. He also said his team needed to go out and win every day of the campaign. "We had a strategy, we stuck to it, we executed it reasonably well. Now, it's in the hands of the voters."

2. *Be Yourself.* Obama wanted to emerge from the campaign—win or lose—as an intact person and not become a parody of himself.

3. *Superhumans.* Some people, such as Hillary Clinton, rise above humanity. She is "beloved and detested, applauded and denounced, famous and infamous, but never ignored."

4. *On Mental Toughness.* Hillary Clinton thought John Kerry "lacked the hardness needed to survive the meat grinder . . . that postmodern politics had become."

5. *Succeeding in the U.S. Senate* . . . requires sublimation of your ego. "Keep your head down. Avoid the limelight. Get on the right committees . . . Do your homework . . . And never forget the care and feeding of the people who sent you . . ."

6. *Take Positions You Believe.* Political candidates must take positions they believe in, because they have to go out and defend those positions every day.

7. *Leverage Your Strengths.* A campaign should be built around a candidate's strengths.

8. *Incumbency.* Incumbents define the political race, even when they are not on the ballot.

9. *"Everybody in Politics Lies . . ."*—the Clintons just had an easier time doing it.

10. *The One Word Answer.* Ask yourself, what is the one word people would use to describe you?

11. *Politicians* . . . should love the art of politics, and they should love people . . . otherwise, why do it?

12. *"All Great Contests Are Head Games"*—Bill Clinton

13. *On Bad Moments.* All politicians have a bad moment in a campaign; it is how you recover that is the key. A politician either finds his voice at a key moment in a campaign, or he does not, and whether he does or not will determine the outcome of the election. Even frontrunners are tested; they do not waltz to the nomination, and how they respond to being tested determines their outcome. For example, Ronald Reagan said that trees cause pollution, and he was still able to win the presidency. Winning candidates follow a hero's narrative: hero stumbles, falls, recovers, comes back, and wins.

14. *Seize the Initiative.* Bill Clinton . . . always wanted to be on the offensive in politics, and if someone got in his way, he just wanted to crush them. He was also blessed with a mind that produced a font of ideas.

Manhunt: The 12-Day Chase for Lincoln's Killer
by James Swanson
(New York: William Morrow, 2006)

Key Insights:

1. *Preparation.* Abraham Lincoln did not speak on a subject of any consequence without a prepared text. He would usually distract and disarm the audience with humor if he was caught in front of people having not prepared.
2. *Naturally Light Hearted.* Lincoln was boyish and fun but the Civil War burdens of his office really wore on him.
3. *Southern Honor.* A true southern man could not be bought; honor was the South's highest virtue.

My FBI: Bringing Down the Mafia,
Investigating Bill Clinton, and Fighting the War on Terror
by Louis J. Freeh with Howard Means
(New York: St. Martin's Press, 2005)

Key Insights:

1. *No Appointments with Royalty.* If you want to see a King, you do not make an appointment. No one is on equal standing with a King; therefore, you have to wait to be summoned by his minions before being granted an audience with him.
2. *FBI Independence.* Congress awards the FBI director with a 10-year tenure to span at least two presidents, which enables independence in the office. Congress also wants to avoid decades-long tenures, such as that served by J. Edgar Hoover, in which it is virtually impossible to remove a director.

3. *Work/Home Balance.* As FBI director, Louis Freeh never believed in working so hard that one forgets his family. The cliché offered by public servants that he or she needs to "spend more time with the family" never rang true with Freeh. To him, "that cliché indicated that the person had probably done both jobs poorly, and (he never) wanted to find (him)self in a position where (he) had to choose between the two." He believes Washington, D.C. is a work-obsessed pathological culture in which people are only happy when the world is in a crisis.

4. *A Father's Public Service Mandate.* Freeh's father told his three sons to serve their nation no matter how difficult, inconvenient, or dangerous the task. Freeh believed passionately in fidelity, courage, and sacrifice as the hallmarks of public service. He knew the FBI did not always achieve those goals on his watch, but he believed it never stopped trying to do so.

5. *Childhood Impressions.* "It's amazing how little classroom moments . . . can color our whole lives."

6. *An Activist Faith.* Freeh believes in an activist faith; it is not only what you believe that matters, it is also what you do about it that counts.

7. *Integrity.* For law enforcement officials, Freeh believed integrity was more important than evidence, or anything else for that matter. "If the people don't trust us, if they don't respect us, then we can have the most impressive evidence in the world and still not win a conviction." Freeh believed a proper law enforcement process was more important than a successful outcome, because the process would stand the test of time and ensure public trust.

8. *Law Enforcement with a Heart.* Freeh allowed a mob boss the opportunity to walk down the street to be arrested rather than have his wife and children witness the act inside their house. The mob boss later repaid Freeh by giving up a larger mob boss in a big case, and he told Freeh he only did it because Freeh afforded him the dignity to save his children from seeing their father arrested.

9. *Drugs, Drugs, Drugs.* Half of all FBI convictions during Freeh's tenure were drug-related cases.

Staying True
by Jenny Sanford
(New York: Ballantine Books, 2010)

<u>Key Insights</u>:

1. *How Small We Are.* "At the beach, I feel wondrously small; my problems are insignificant in the big, beautiful world."

2. *Love Is . . .* "more than a feeling—it's an action you engage in every day through the things you do for those you cherish. Values and common goals sustain you with those you love. A happy marriage is to have a partner who thinks more of you than you do of yourself."

3. *Success Is . . .* "a personal thing defined by the way you live your life every day, and by what you do with the skills and blessings you have bestowed on you." "What matters most is how you live your life, not what you have to show for it."

4. *A Successful Congressional Campaign.* Governor Mark Sanford's first congressional campaign was built on his principles and values—he would have rather lost

the campaign than sacrificed his principles. He raised as much money as possible and saved it until the end, when regular voters would decide for whom they would vote. He liked the notion of term limits—you serve for a while and then go back home and live under the laws you enacted.

Hot, Flat, and Crowded: Why We Need a Green Revolution—and How It Can Renew America by Thomas Friedman (New York: Farrar, Straus, and Giroux, 2008)

Key Insights:

1. *On Change.* "If we want things to stay as they are, things will have to change."
2. *Why America Was Great.* "America was a country that was always reinventing itself . . . because it was a country that always welcomed all kinds of oddballs and . . . had this wonderful spirit of openness. American openness has always been an inspiration for the whole world . . . If you go dark, the world goes dark."
3. *America's Slow Erosion?* Fareed Zakaria says the American political system may not be able to handle society's big problems. On big issues no one wants to be the guy who takes the hit, so the buck keeps getting passed until we collectively implode as a country. American society may slowly erode—schools decline, science research and development fades, immigration is choked off . . . The danger will be that things will go along until one day they do not, and we will wake up to find our country has fallen apart.

4. *Inflection Points Are Hard to Spot.* The changes that started the Industrial Revolution did not get recognized right away. Winners and losers were only identified after some time. Similarly, September 11, 2001 was a big event that illuminated a whole set of trends that had been building for a long time.

5. *Get the Big Things Right.* If you get the big three or four things right in life, the rest of life falls in line. For example, after World War II, the world focused on human rights, quality of life, and prevention of another world war. With those big issues being pushed, the rest of the agenda fell into line and the world generally prospered.

"The Science of Insurgency Can Shape Our Strategy" by Dan Vergano (*USA Today*, December 22, 2009)

Key Insight:

1. *Terror Signals.* Just as financial traders observe the trades of others as indications to buy or sell securities, insurgent groups view the attacks of others as signals for them to instigate their own attacks. Each attack is a trigger for the next attack without having any hierarchy coordinating the attacks.

The Politician: An Insider's Account of John Edwards's Pursuit of the Presidency and the Scandal That Brought Him Down
by Andrew Young
(New York: St. Martin's Press, 2010)

Key Insights:

1. *Life Is a Roller Coaster.* "Life inevitably brings change, loss, and trauma to everyone." After John Edwards's son died in a car crash, Edwards learned to "control his own expectations and never take anything for granted."

2. *Think Big.* "Wealthy, powerful men don't think small . . ."

3. *Don't Believe the Hype.* John Edwards loved the attention he got as a politician, but he was always wary. "They build you up so they can tear you down."

4. *Traveler's Blues.* "Like many people who travel for work, the senator would complain about how much life 'sucked' because he was often away from home."

5. *A Common Touch.* Edwards came from humble roots and made a point to go out of his way to say hello to and thank back room cooks, attendants, and others.

6. *And Then What?* "He didn't say what he intended to do if he became president, . . . but most big-time politicians don't think much about what they will do when they get to the top of the mountain until they arrive. Until then, it's all about the climb." Although he had the necessary "likability" quality people want in a President, Edwards never had a concrete answer to the question: "Why do you want to be President?" He had no grand vision or big policy ideas.

7. *A Natural.* Edwards looked, talked, and acted like a leader.
8. *Seize the Moment.* When a crack of opportunity opens, you have to jump at it even if you are not completely ready, because big chances do not come along often.
9. *The Battle Lines.* In a political campaign, things inevitably end up being viewed as good versus evil.
10. *A Positive Outlook.* Cynics do not build anything; optimists do.
11. *Perfection Is Unattainable.* Be a "big you" instead of a "little Jesus." You cannot try to be perfect and then beat yourself up when you fail.

The Ghost Writer
by Robert Harris
(New York: Simon and Schuster, 2007)

Key Insights:

1. *A Different Type of Politician.* "Everybody voted for him. He wasn't a politician; he was a craze." "This was his genius: to refresh and elevate the clichés of politics by the sheer force of his performance."
2. *What Fascinates in Politics.* People are not grabbed by policy. "What fascinates people is always people—the details of another person's life."
3. *The First Rule of Politics.* Never lose touch with your base. You need to reach beyond your base, but never lose touch with it altogether.
4. *The Successful Person's Focus.* "People who succeed in life are rarely reflective. Their gaze is always on the future: that's why they succeed. It's not in their nature to remember what they were feeling, or wearing . . ."

5. *The Guy Behind the Politician*. "He looks exactly like the sort of unappealing inadequate who is congenitally drawn to politics . . . a greasy engineer in the boiler room of power."

6. *When Leaders Really Led*. "There was a time . . . when princes taking their countries to war were supposed to risk their lives in battle—you know, lead by example. Now they travel around in bombproof cars and make fortunes 3,000 miles away, while the rest of us are stuck with the consequences of their actions."

7. *Why Ghost Writers Are Successful*. "A ghost who has only a lay knowledge of the subject will be able to keep asking the same questions as the lay reader, and will therefore open up the potential readership of the book to a much wider audience."

8. *What Sells*. Big names do not sell books, music, or movies—*heart* does.

9. *Understand What You Can*. If Jesus could not sort out all of the world's problems, do not imagine that you can.

10. *On Power*. "It isn't having power that's exhausting—it's not having it that wears you out."

CHAPTER 9:
SPORTS AND ENTERTAINMENT

"You can't fake dedication. Or talent. Not for long anyway."

—Rich Eisen

I Never Left Home
by Bob Hope
(New York: Simon and Schuster, 1944)

Key Insights:

1. *A Changed Perspective.* After he returned from a year entertaining the troops in World War II, Bob Hope said, "I came home to find people still living and thinking the way I lived and thought before I was given a look at sacrifice . . . Until a lot more of us realize what our men have gone through in planes and tanks . . . it's going to be tough to talk to the men coming back. And in the case of those who aren't doing all they should, it's going to be tougher to look them in the eye."

2. *On Waiting to Deploy.* "It isn't exactly as if you're scared. But it isn't exactly as if you're not."

3. *Respect Versus Rank.* "Rank meant what the men thought of you, not what was on your shoulders."

4. *Entertainment's Role in War.* "For a little while, they were able to forget completely their own problems and what they'd been through, or what they might be expecting to go through.

5. *Why Hollywood Should Support the Troops.* "Playing the European Theater, or any theater of war, is a good thing for actors. It's a way of showing us that there's something more important than billing; or how high your (rating) is; or breaking the house record in Denver."

Total Access: A Journey to the Center of the NFL Universe by Rich Eisen (New York: Thomas Dunne Books, 2007)

Key Insights:

1. *Follow Your Passion* . . . because you cannot succeed at something you do not like.

2. *Relax in the Moment.* Sterling Sharpe said of fellow NFL great, Brett Favre, "When I got to play with him, I had been in the league four years . . . and football wasn't fun. It was a job. And then to watch Brett come in the huddle and notice people in the stands and say, 'Hey, have you eaten at this restaurant?' You know, things that were the farthest away from trying to pick up a first down and score a touchdown. It relaxed you and allowed you to go out and make football fun again. That was probably the most important thing that I took away from the game after playing with him was the fact that it was never a job. It was never a business. It was always fun."

3. *Dreams Versus Goals.* NFL Hall of Famer, Emmitt Smith said, "My high school coach always told the team that it's only a dream until you write it down—then, it becomes a goal." Smith followed that advice and wrote a list of team and personal goals before each season began, and he would track his progress against that list. He is the NFL's all-time leading rusher.

Game of Kings: A Year Among the Oddballs and Geniuses Who Make Up America's Top High School Chess Team by Michael Weinreb (New York: Gotham, 2007)

Key Insights:

1. *On Mental Development.* "You see things when your mind is developing that you don't see when you get older ... chess is all about seeing things no one else sees, which is why it's a sport that always produced its share of prodigies ..."
2. *Humility and Chess.* "It takes time to realize that most chess players, like many artists, are constantly bounding between . . . self-importance and self-flagellation." Overconfidence kills potentially great chess players. "Even the top echelon of players often maintain a base of humility beneath their bluster," because there is always someone better out there.
3. *No Dumb Luck.* "Chess is a sport of actions and reactions, and without a rudimentary knowledge of strategy and tactics, the two primary elements of the game, it is virtually impossible to extend the game beyond a couple of dozen moves. There is no such thing as dumb luck." "In the end, luck gives way to strategy."

4. *Chess Strategy*. Garry Kasparov said, "Chess is a mixture of sport, psychological warfare, science, and art." "The middle game is where theory and memorization of certain lines of attack often give way to innovation and improvisation, where thought must be given to the value of every exchange of material, and where the board slowly begins to simplify, until the queens are usually off the board and there are only a few pieces left, and the middle game transitions into the endgame. By then, one player often has an edge, and it is this player's job to exploit this edge, to turn an advantage in material or an advantage in position into victory, while the player with lesser material or a less developed position does all he can to stave off defeat."

5. *Visualizing the Board.* Great chess players do not visualize many moves in advance; they cannot do it simply due to the number of possibilities. "Grandmasters, in certain cases, can think ahead eight or nine moves on a specific line or tactic . . . The rest of the game is often dictated by feel; once you know the fundamentals of the game, you see a position and you can eliminate the moves that don't make sense."

6. *Chess Success.* "Willy started playing chess, and after that, he never stopped. Something clicked. Willy is no better than an average student, but here was something at which he could achieve tangible success. He started playing in tournaments nearly every weekend. He started taking home trophies."

7. *Bobby Fischer's Preparations.* The difference between being pretty good and really great in chess is preparation. "Bobby Fischer had become terminally obsessed with the game at the age of six, and entered his first tournament at age nine, and when he wasn't home, buried in chess

literature, he spent most of his time (playing the game)." "The evolution took place despite the growing dismay of his mother, who consulted experts and pleaded with psychiatrists and eventually gave up and left her boy to fend for himself in their Brooklyn apartment, surrounded by his books and his boards." Fischer's studies led to great innovative moves, such as his stunning sacrifice of his queen on the 17th move that *Chess Review* referred to as the game of the century. To become a Bobby Fischer, "it requires something more than devotion, something more than commitment; it requires love. And this love cannot be forced. And this love must be coupled with other attributes, such as stamina and the ability to withstand defeat, which means the ability to overcome self-doubt . . . If you have a winning game and you lose it, you should come home and not be able to sleep at night."

8. *Psychology of Chess*. "The thing about being a good player is you can't be hypocritical . . . Under the pressure, if you have some psychological bubble, something you haven't dealt with, it's going to come up. If you're addicted to comfort in any way, you can't be a good chess player. You have to be at peace with chess." Also, "to be a good player, you've got to be a fighter . . . Playing at the park can really toughen you up. You have to deal with all the banter, figure out how not to get hustled; it's good for concentration, too."

9. *Chess Personalities*. "The best players on our team . . . are a little bit strange. "If you're involved in an academic endeavor, there's something appealing about building yourself up to be so weird and unreachable, you know? It's like Einstein: You want to differentiate yourself. You want to become a legend, so you make up something

like how you don't remember where your own house is, you have to ask someone on the street. And you take on a life larger than yourself. It's easy to do if you're doing something difficult."

10. *Chess Benefits*. Good high school chess players "have already gotten the value (of chess) . . . Their lives have already been made much better. They're already better problem solvers. They're already tougher mentally. They're already more creative. They have more things to draw on to get them through the difficulties in life. The benefit will last for the rest of their lives."

Moving the Chains: Tom Brady and the Pursuit of Everything by Charles Pierce (New York: Farrar, Straus, and Giroux, 2006)

Key Insights:

1. *Heroes* . . . need something to save, as indicated in Bertolt Brecht's *Galileo*: "Andrea: Unhappy is the land that breeds no hero. Galileo: No, Andrea. Unhappy is the land that needs a hero."

2. *"Destiny Doesn't Always Walk a Straight Line."* When Tom Brady was a college freshman, he walked into a Michigan diner with all of the football greats on the wall. His mother recalls, "He told me that, one day, he was going to have people in that place know who he was." Brady did not set records at the University of Michigan, but he would win many championships with the New England Patriots, and everyone in that diner knows who he is.

3. *Work Harder.* Tom Brady always had a notion that if he did not improve, his career would end, which actually

has given him an edge over quarterbacks who have always had things handed to them. He was not highly recruited out of high school. He shared playing time at Michigan with another quarterback, and he had to fight frustration, stay on track, and avoid getting sidetracked by decisions out of his control. He was not drafted until the NFL's sixth round.

4. *Practice the Little Things.* "Why do you work on these little things? Because they ain't little. They get big pretty quick." In his first Super Bowl, Brady felt very comfortable because he had studied so much film prior to the game that he knew what to expect of his opponent.

5. *Don't Be a Follower.* "The pull of the pack is to act in a certain way … and (Brady) wouldn't do it. He took things seriously, and he was very gracious, so I figured, here was a guy who was going to go through the football program and then go find a life for himself." "It was strange to see played out on a vast stage the same thing that happened in that classroom of knuckleheads … It was very strange to see what had become of the kid who always brought the books to class and who was never given any shit about it, even from the people who—whether they knew it or not—already were dedicating their lives to giving shit to people about things like that. Because there was something about him that connected. Because there was something about this Brady character that was real." "He will be smart and handsome and rich and popular and he will be one of the guys, too. He will move the chains in his life, constantly, so that he will determine its ultimate destiny."

6. *A Guy Who Cares.* "If you ever hear him talking to anyone . . . it's always, 'How's your job?' That's always

been part of his being a teammate. It's just such a part of his personality. I mean, it's not just his work. He's incredibly loving." "He's a very caring individual . . . when he talks to you, you feel like you're the only person in the room, you know?"

7. *"He Fit All the Categories That Were Hard to Define."* You can't always judge someone's ability on a form or through a test. "There was something about Tom Brady . . . even though it wasn't anything he could time with a stopwatch or write down on a three-by-five card. There was no line on any form for loyalty or devotion, or the kind of charisma that engenders either one." "People recruit and sign people in a box . . . That box doesn't include the intangibles of playing a position. People draft safely."

8. *Why He Was Drafted.* The New England Patriots did not view Brady as a franchise quarterback—they were not clairvoyant in being able to see that a part-time college quarterback might blossom into one of the NFL's all-time greats. Coach Bill Belichick said, "Our vision wasn't that Tom was our franchise quarterback but that Tom had been in situations—both in playing-time and game-management situations, and tight games against good competition—and he'd handled all of them pretty well."

9. *Why the Patriots Franchise Works.* Owner Bob Craft wanted the Patriots to be a family values operation in a business that is extremely competitive, "where it often becomes necessary to cast out members of the 'family' when they become too old or injured to carry their weight, or when their salaries become too high for the 'family budget.'" The goal was to always try and do things in a way that would bring the community

together and run the team in a certain dignified way. Craft says, "We've tried to set a value system of things we'd accept and things we wouldn't accept."

10. *Bloom Where Planted.* As a rookie, Brady caught offensive coordinator Charlie Weis's attention. Watching Brady with the rookies, Weis noticed that these second tier players got better. Weis said, "Brady had taken what he had been given, and out of it, he was crafting a team around him . . . It wasn't that they could all play. You just watched them all mature because he would always strive to be the best there, because he'd work harder than anyone else in the weight room . . . If somebody ran something wrong, he'd correct them. He developed an understanding not only of his position but of the entire offense. In his leadership style, he was able to do that."

11. *On Luck.* There is some luck involved in winning as many Super Bowls as Tom Brady has. The AFC East Division was poor for many of those years, so the Patriots simply had more shots at the playoffs than most teams.

12. *Lifelong Learning.* Brady is an endlessly curious learner. He likes to understand how things work, which is why he is so good at breaking down defenses and finding their weaknesses. He also studies other successful people and how they put their lives together to make it all work.

13. *Financial Ruin.* "78 percent of NFL players are unemployed, bankrupt, or divorced within two years of leaving the game."

The Essential Wooden
by John Wooden and Steve Jamison
(New York: McGraw-Hill, 2007)

<u>Key Insights</u>:

1. *Setting Your Own Standard.* Reach your own highest level of success; do not measure yourself against an opponent. The battle is within you, and if you do your best and lose the game, that is better than winning with less than your best effort.
2. *Wooden's Life Mantra.* "Live as though you'll die tomorrow. Learn as though you'll live forever."
3. *Wooden's Life Lessons.* Never lie, cheat, or steal; and do not whine, complain, or make excuses.
4. *On Controlling Anger.* Abraham Lincoln said, "There is nothing stronger than gentleness . . . It takes strength inside to be gentle on the outside." Wooden received only two technical fouls in his 40-year coaching career. Win or lose, he tried to maintain the same behavior. Emotional highs and lows lead to bad judgments.
5. *Be True to Yourself.* "Be willing to suffer the consequences of standing up for your beliefs."
6. *Don't Flinch at Failure.* Act, initiate, and be bold rather than hang back in fear of failure. "When it's time to pull the trigger, you must do it."
7. *Don't Worry.* Worrying about life is wasting energy. Concern is okay, because it focuses you to take action to alleviate that concern.
8. *Only Words.* Let both praise and criticism wash off of you.
9. *Watch What You Say.* "Saying things about others is a bad habit."

10. *On Luck.* Branch Rickey said, "Luck is the residue of design." Hard work is the key; there are no shortcuts in life.

11. *No Free Rides.* "Tough work makes you tougher. A free ride isn't free."

12. *Character Counts.* "Ability may get you to the top, but it takes character to stay there."

13. *Learn from Everyone.* Abraham Lincoln said, "You can learn something from every person you meet—even if it's what not to do."

14. *People Talk.* People will talk about you no matter what you do, so you might as well do the right thing.

15. *Pressure Versus Stress.* Pressure is healthy and leads to improvement. Stress is unhealthy and leads to mistakes.

16. *Practice Hard.* Wooden was efficient with his practices and lived by the mantra, "Failing to prepare is preparing to fail." There was no time wasted, no long practices. Pressure in practice was designed to make the games seem easy by comparison. His entire practice was scripted.

17. *Perfection Is Impossible.* Capitalizing on imperfection makes all the difference.

18. *Deliver Knowledge in Bite-Sized Increments.* It makes it easier for a student to swallow.

19. *Competition = 50% Fight + 50% Knowledge.*

20. *No Bad Apples.* Get rid of even one person who does not align with your values, or he will ruin your team.

21. *Take the Stage.* Sometimes leaders have to be good actors.

Undertaker's Son: Life Lessons from a Coach
by Richard "Digger" Phelps with Jack Colwell
(Lyons Press, 2010)

<u>Key Insights</u>:

1. *Visualizing Success.* As a basketball coach, Digger Phelps had his players cut down the nets prior to a big game to mentally visualize and become comfortable with victory. He created an expectation of winning.
2. *Dare to Dream.* A dream drives you to succeed, but since all dreams do not work out, Phelps believes you should have a backup plan. Phelps realized his dreams by working hard and networking with key people to open doors of opportunity.
3. *Highlight Yourself.* Phelps says, "He who does not toot his own horn has his horn tooted."
4. *Don't Cheat.* Phelps was willing to lose players to unscrupulous coaches rather than sacrifice his own integrity by cheating the rules.
5. *Be There on the Ground.* When Phelps ran "Operation Weed and Seed" for the President of the United States, he went to the rough neighborhoods. A leader cannot just be about pomp and ceremony.
6. *On Images.* "It's just a fact that when an image begins to stick, rightly or wrongly, actions that enhance that image become more significant."
7. *Simple Messages Win.* Do not get sidetracked by flaps or side issues. For example, the simplest campaign message, "It's the economy, stupid," trumped everything else in Bill Clinton's successful presidential campaign.
8. *Ronald Reagan's Awe-Inspiring Farewell Speech.* "Whatever else history may say about me when I'm

211

gone, I hope it will record that I appealed to your best hopes, not your worst fears, to your confidence rather than your doubts."

9. *Admit Your Fears* . . . because it would be crazy not to.

LIST OF SOURCES

Ackroyd, Peter. *Newton*. New York: Doubleday, 2006.

Aliber, Robert. *Your Money and Your Life: A Lifetime Approach to Money Management*. Stanford, California: Stanford Economics and Finance, 2010.

Allen, Paul. *Idea Man: A Memoir by the Cofounder of Microsoft*. New York: Penguin Books, 2011.

Alpert, Mark. *Final Theory*. New York: Touchstone, 2008.

Anderson, Chris. *Free: How Today's Smartest Businesses Profit by Giving Something for Nothing*. New York: Hyperion, 2009.

Archer, Jeffrey. *False Impression*. New York: St. Martin's Press, 2006.

Archer, Jeffrey. *Kane and Abel*. New York: St. Martin's Press, 1979.

Archer, Jeffrey. *A Matter of Honor*. New York: Pocket Books, 1987.

Archer, Jeffrey. *Paths of Glory*. New York: St. Martin's Press, 2009.

Archer, Jeffrey. *Twelve Red Herrings*. New York: HarperCollins, 1994.

Baldacci, David. *The Collectors*. New York: Hachette Book Group, 2006.

Barclay, Linwood. *Fear the Worst*. New York: Dell, 2010.

Barclay, Linwood. *Lone Wolf*. New York: Bantam Books, 2006.

Barclay, Linwood. *Never Look Away*. New York: Dell, 2011.

Barclay, Linwood. *No Time for Goodbye*. New York: Bantam Books, 2007.

Barclay, Linwood. *Too Close To Home*. New York: Bantam Books, 2009.

Barton, Bruce. *The Man Nobody Knows: The Modern Life of Jesus Christ*. Charter, 1962.

Bass, Jefferson. *Carved in Bone*. New York: Harper, 2006.

Berenson, Alex. *The Ghost War*. New York: The Penguin Group, 2008.

Berman, Karen and Joe Knight with John Case. *Financial Intelligence: A Manager's Guide to Knowing What the Numbers Really Mean*. Boston: Harvard Business School Press, 2006.

Blumenthal, Karen. *Grande Expectations: A Year in the Life of Starbucks' Stock*. New York: Three Rivers Press, 2007.

Bordain, Anthony. *The Nasty Bits*. New York: Bloomsbury, 2006.

Branson, Richard. *Business Stripped Bare*. London: Virgin Books, 2008.

Brennan, Allison. *Cutting Edge*. New York: Ballantine Books, 2009.

Brennan, Allison. *Fear No Evil*. New York: Ballantine Books, 2007.

Brown, Dan. *The Lost Symbol*. New York: Anchor Books, 2009.

Browne, Sylvia. *The Mystical Life of Jesus: An Uncommon Perspective on the Life of Christ*. New York: Penguin Group, 2006.

Cassidy, John. *How Markets Fail: The Logic of Economic Calamities*. New York: Farrar, Straus, and Giroux, 2009.

Cerasini, Marc. *24 Declassified: Operation Hell Gate*. New York: Harper Entertainment, 2005.

Child, Lee. *Gone Tomorrow*. New York: Dell, 2010.

Child, Lee. *Nothing to Lose*. New York: Dell, 2010.

Chua, Amy. *Battle Hymn of the Tiger Mother*. New York: The Penguin Press, 2011.

Coben, Harlan. *Gone for Good*. New York: Dell, 2003.

Coben, Harlan. *Hold Tight*. New York: Penguin Books, 2008.

Coben, Harlan. *The Final Detail*. New York: Dell Publishing, 1999.

Compton, Jodi. *The 37th Hour*. New York: Dell, 2005.

Connelly, Michael. *The Brass Verdict*. London: Orion Books, 2008.

Covert, Jack and Todd Satterstein. *The 100 Best Business Books of All-Time*. New York: The Penguin Group, 2009.

Crabbe, Richard. *Hell's Gate*. New York: Thomas Dunne Books, 2008.

Cramer, James J. with Cliff Mason. *Getting Back to Even*. New York: Simon and Schuster, 2009.

Crescenzi, Anthony. *The Strategic Bond Investor: Strategies and Tools to Unlock the Power of the Bond Market*. New York: McGraw-Hill, 2010.

Crais, Robert. *The First Rule*. New York: G. P. Putnam's Sons, 2010.

Crichton, Michael. *The Great Train Robbery*. New York: HarperCollins, 1975.

Crocker III, H. W. *Triumph: The Power and the Glory of the Catholic Church: A 2,000-Year History*. Roseville, California: Prima, 2001.

Cussler, Clive. *Inca Gold*. New York: Pocket Star Books, 1994.

Deaver, Jeffery. *The Burning Wire*. New York: Simon and Schuster, 2010.

Deaver, Jeffery. *Carte Blanche*. New York: Simon and Schuster, 2011.

Deaver, Jeffery. *Edge*. New York: Simon and Schuster, 2010.

Deaver, Jeffery. *More Twisted: Collected Stories, Volume II*. New York: Pocket Books, 2006.

Deaver, Jeffery. *Roadside Crosses*. New York: Simon and Schuster, 2010.

Deaver, Jeffery, et al. *Watchlist*. New York: Vanguard Press, 2009.

Dekker, Ted. *Boneman's Daughters*. New York: Center Street, 2009.

Dekker, Ted. *The Bride Collector*. New York: Center Street, 2010.

Dekker, Ted. *The Priest's Graveyard*. New York: Center Street, 2011.

Dekker, Ted. *Saint*. Nashville, Tennessee: WestBow Press, 2006.

Dekker, Ted. *Skin*. Brentwood, Tennessee: Thomas Nelson, 2007.

Diefendorf, Elizabeth. *The New York Public Library's Books of the Century*. Oxford, England: Oxford University Press, 1997.

Dietrich, William. *The Barbary Pirates*. New York: HarperCollins, 2010.

Eisen, Rich. *Total Access: A Journey to the Center of the NFL Universe*. New York: Thomas Dunne Books, 2007.

El-Arian, Mohammad. Interview Notes with PIMCO CEO. Date Unknown.

Erdman, Paul. *The Crash of '79*. Berkeley, California: Berkeley Press, 1988.

Finder, Joseph. *Buried Secrets*. New York: St. Martin's Press, 2011.

Finder, Joseph. *High Crimes*. New York: Avon Books, 1998.

Finder, Joseph. *Vanished*. New York: St. Martin's Press, 2009.

Fink, Anne-Marie. *The Money Makers: How Extraordinary Managers Win in a World Turned Upside Down*. New York: Crown Business, 2009.

Follett, Ken. *Code to Zero*. New York: Signet, 2001.

Follett, Ken. *A Dangerous Fortune*. New York: Dell, 1993.

Follett, Ken. *Eye of the Needle*. New York: HarperCollins, 1978.

Follett, Ken. *Fall of Giants*. New York: MacMillan, 2011.

Follett, Ken. *Jackdaws*. New York: Penguin Books, 2001.

Follett, Ken. *The Key to Rebecca*. New York: Signet, 1980.

Follett, Ken. *The Shakeout*. New York: The Armchair Detective Library, 1990.

Follett, Ken. *World Without End*. New York: Dutton, 2007.

Franzen, Jonathan. *The Corrections*. New York: Picador, 2001.

Freeh, Louis with Howard Means. *My FBI: Bringing Down the Mafia, Investigating Bill Clinton, and Fighting the War on Terror*. New York: St. Martin's Press, 2005.

Frey, Stephen. *Hell's Gate*. New York: Atria Books, 2009.

Friedman, George. *The Next Decade: Where We've Been . . . and Where We're Going*. New York: Doubleday, 2011.

Friedman, Thomas. *Hot, Flat, and Crowded: Why We Need a Green Revolution—and How It Can Renew America.* New York: Farrar, Straus, and Giroux, 2008.

Gaiman, Neil. *American Gods.* New York: Perennial, 2003.

Garland, Alex. *The Beach.* New York: Riverhead Books, 1999.

Gawande, Atul. *The Checklist Manifesto: How to Get Things Right.* New York: Metropolitan Books, 2009.

Gingrich, Newt and William Forstchen. *To Try Men's Souls: A Novel of George Washington and the Fight for American Freedom.* New York: Thomas Dunne Books, 2009.

Gladwell, Malcolm. *What the Dog Saw.* New York: Little, Brown, and Company, 2009.

Greenspan, Alan. *The Age of Turbulence: Adventures in a New World.* New York: Penguin Books, 2007.

Griffin, W. E. B. and William Butterworth. *The Double Agents.* G. P. Putnam's Sons, 2007.

Grisham, John. *The Associate.* New York: Dell, 2009.

Grisham, John. *The Confession.* New York: Dell, 2010.

Grisham, John. *Ford County: Stories.* New York: Bantam Books, 2009.

Gross, Andrew. *Reckless*. New York: Harper, 2010.

Harris, Robert. *The Ghost Writer*. New York: Simon and Schuster, 2007.

Hayes, Kevin. *The Road to Monticello: The Life and Mind of Thomas Jefferson*. New York: Oxford University Press, 2008.

Heilemann, John and Mark Halperin. *Game Change: Obama and the Clintons, McCain and Palin, and the Race of a Lifetime*. New York: HarperCollins, 2010.

Heraclitus. Translated by Brooks Haxton. *Fragments: The Collected Wisdom of Heraclitus*. New York: Viking Press, 2001.

Hope, Bob. *I Never Left Home*. New York: Simon and Schuster, 1944.

Isaacson, Walter. *American Sketches: Great Leaders, Creative Thinkers, and Heroes of a Hurricane*. New York: Simon and Schuster, 2009.

Jackson, Lisa. *Born to Die*. New York: Zebra Books, 2011.

James Au, Wagner. *The Making of Second Life*. New York: Collins, 2008.

Jarvis, Jeff. *What Would Google Do?* New York: Collins Business, 2009.

Javers, Eamon. *Broker, Trader, Lawyer, Spy: The Secret World of Corporate Espionage*. New York: HarperCollins, 2010.

Kahney, Leander. *Inside Steve's Brain*. New York: Portfolio, 2008.

Kanon, Joseph. *The Good German*. New York: Picador, 2006.

Kazdin, Alan. *The Kazdin Method for Parenting the Defiant Child*. New York: Mariner Books, 2008.

Kendall, Joshua. *The Man Who Made Lists*. New York: G. P. Putnam's Sons, 2008.

Kessler, Ronald. *In the President's Secret Service*. New York: Three Rivers Press, 2009.

Khoury, Raymond. *The Sanctuary*. New York: Signet, 2008.

King, Stephen. *Cell*. New York: Pocket Books, 2006.

King, Stephen. *Everything's Eventual*. New York: Pocket Books, 2002.

Kirn, Walter. *Up in the Air*. New York: Doubleday, 2001.

Krakauer, Jon. *Into the Wild*. New York: Anchor Books, 1996.

Kurzweil, Ray. *The Singularity Is Near: When Humans Transcend Biology*. New York: Viking, 2005.

Kuzneski, Chris. *Sign of the Cross*. New York: Jove Books, 2006.

Labriola, Jerry. *The Strange Death of Napoleon Bonaparte.* New York: Strong Books, 2007.

Landsburg, Steven. *The Big Questions: Tackling the Problems of Philosophy with Ideas from Mathematics, Economics, and Physics.* New York: Free Press, 2009.

Larson, Erik. *The Devil in the White City: Murder, Magic, and Madness at the Fair That Changed America.* New York: Vintage Books, 2003.

Larson, Erik. *Thunderstruck.* New York: Crown Publishers, 2006.

Larsson, Stieg. *The Girl Who Played with Fire.* New York: Vintage Books, 2009.

Lashinsky, Adam. "The Decade of Steve (Jobs): His Legacy." *Fortune.* November 23, 2009.

Lehane, Dennis. *The Given Day.* New York: William Morrow, 2008.

Lescroat, John. *Betrayal.* New York: Dutton, 2008.

Lewis, Michael. *The Big Short: Inside the Doomsday Machine.* New York: W. W. Norton and Company, 2010.

Levitt, Steven and Stephen Dubner. *SuperFreakonomics: Global Cooling, Patriotic Prostitutes, and Why Suicide Bombers Should Buy Life Insurance.* New York: HarperLuxe, 2009.

Liss, David. *The Devil's Company*. New York: Ballantine Books, 2009.

Ludlum, Robert. *The Ambler Warning*. New York: St. Martin's Press, 2005.

Lynn, Matthew. *Bust: Greece, the Euro, and the Sovereign Debt Crisis*. New Jersey: John Wiley and Sons, 2011.

Ma, Jeffrey. *The House Advantage: Playing the Odds to Win Big in Business*. New York: Palgrave MacMillan, 2010.

Marks, Howard. *The Most Important Thing: Uncommon Sense for the Thoughtful Investor*. New York: Columbia University Press, 2011.

Martin, William. *The Lost Constitution*. New York: Tom Doherty Associates, 2007.

McTaggert, Lynne. *The Field: The Quest for the Secret Force of the Universe*. London: HarperCollins, 2001.

Meltzer, Brad. *Dead Even*. New York: William Morrow, 1998.

Meltzer, Brad. *The First Counsel*. New York: Warner Books, 2001.

Meltzer, Brad. *The Inner Circle*. New York: Grand Central Publishing, 2011.

Meyer, Stephanie. *Eclipse*. New York: Little, Brown, and Company, 2007.

Meyer, Stephanie. *New Moon*. New York: Little, Brown, and Company, 2006.

Meyer, Stephanie. *Twilight*. New York: Little, Brown, and Company, 2005.

Mezrich, Ben. *Fertile Ground*. New York: Avon, 2001.

Miller, Joel. *The Revolutionary Paul Revere*. Nashville: Thomas Nelson, 2010.

Moscowitz, Tobias and L. Jon Wertheim. *Scorecasting: The Hidden Influences Behind How Sports Are Played and Games Are Won*. New York: Crown Archetype, 2011.

Moss Kanter, Rosabeth. *Confidence: How Winning Streaks and Losing Streaks Begin and End*. New York: Three Rivers Press, 2004.

Palmer, Michael. *The Second Opinion*. New York: St. Martin's Press, 2009.

Patterson, James. *1ˢᵗ to Die*. New York: Warner Books, 2001.

Patterson, James and Michael Ledwidge. *Run for Your Life*. New York: Little, Brown, and Company, 2009.

Patterson, James and Maxine Paetro. *4ᵗʰ of July*. New York: Little, Brown, and Company, 2005.

Patterson, Richard North. *Degree of Guilt*. New York: St. Martin's Press, 1992.

Patterson, Richard North. *The Spire*. New York: Henry Holt and Company, 2009.

Phelps, Richard "Digger" Phelps with Jack Colwell. *Undertaker's Son: Life Lessons from a Coach*. Lyons Press, 2010.

Pierce, Charles. *Moving the Chains: Tom Brady and the Pursuit of Everything*. New York: Farrar, Straus, and Giroux, 2006.

Rachman, Tom. *The Imperfectionists*. New York: Dial Press, 2010.

Reich, Christopher. *Rules of Deception*. New York: First Anchor Books, 2008.

Reich, Christopher. *Rules of Vengeance*. New York: Random House, 2009.

Reich, Robert. *Aftershock: The Next Economy and America's Failure*. New York: Vintage Books, 2010.

Ridley, Matt. *The Rational Optimist: How Prosperity Evolves*. New York: HarperCollins, 2010.

Ridpath, Michael. *Final Venture*. New York: Penguin Books, 2001.

Robbins, David. *The Betrayal Game*. New York: Bantam Books, 2009.

Sanford, Jenny. *Staying True*. New York: Ballantine Books, 2010.

Sanford, John. *Dark of the Moon*. New York: G. P. Putnam's Sons, 2007.

Sanford, John. *Phantom Prey*. New York: G. P. Putnam's Sons, 2008.

Sanford, John. *Wicked Prey*. New York: G. P. Putnam's Sons, 2009.

Schwed, Fred. *Where Are All the Customers' Yachts?: Or A Good Hard Look at Wall Street*. New York: Simon and Schuster, 1940.

Scott, James. *Seeing Like a State: How Certain Schemes to Improve the Human Condition Have Failed*. New Haven: Yale University Press, 1998.

Shepard, Adam. *Scratch Beginnings: Me, $25, and the Search for the American Dream*. New York: Harper, 2008.

Sierra, Javier. *The Secret Supper*. New York: Atria Books, 2004.

Silva, Daniel. *Moscow Rules*. New York: G. P. Putnam's Sons, 2008.

Simpson, Mona. *A Regular Guy*. New York: Vintage Books, 1996.

Swanson, James. *Manhunt: The 12-Day Chase for Lincoln's Killer*. New York: William Morrow, 2006.

Tapply, William. *Shadow of Death*. New York: St. Martin's Press, 2001.

Tett, Gillian. *Fool's Gold: How the Bold Dream of a Small Tribe at J.P Morgan Was Corrupted by Wall Street Greed and Unleashed a Catastrophe*. New York: Free Press, 2009.

Thor, Brad. *The First Commandment*. London: Pocket Books, 2007.

Thor, Brad. *The Last Patriot*. New York: Pocket Books, 2008.

Unger, Lisa. *Beautiful Lies*. New York: Vintage Books, 2008.

Van Lustbader, Eric. *Robert Ludlum's The Bourne Sanction*. New York: Grand Central Publishing, 2008.

Verdon, John. *Think of a Number*. New York: Broadway Paperbacks, 2010.

Vergano, Dan. "The Science of Insurgency Can Shape Our Strategy." *USA Today*, December 22, 2009.

Weinreb, Michael. *Game of Kings: A Year Among the Oddballs and Geniuses Who Make Up America's Top High School Chess Team*. New York: Gotham, 2007.

Wheelan, Charles. *Naked Economics: Undressing the Dismal Science*. New York: W. W. Norton and Company, 2010.

White, Stephen. *The Program*. New York: Dell, 2001.

Wolfe, Tom. *I Am Charlotte Simmons*. New York: Farrar, Straus, and Giroux, 2004.

Wooden, John and Steve Jamison. *The Essential Wooden*. New York: McGraw-Hill, 2007.

Yessayan, Raffi. *Eight in the Box*. New York: Ballantine Books, 2010.

Young, Andrew. *The Politician: An Insider's Account of John Edwards's Pursuit of the Presidency and the Scandal That Brought Him Down*. New York: St. Martin's Press, 2010.